SCIENCE AND MEDICAL DISCOVERIES

Germs

Beth Donovan Reh, *Book Editor*

Bruce Glassman, *Vice President*
Bonnie Szumski, *Publisher*
Helen Cothran, *Managing Editor*
David M. Haugen, *Series Editor*

GREENHAVEN PRESS
An imprint of Thomson Gale, a part of The Thomson Corporation

THOMSON
™
GALE

Detroit • New York • San Francisco • San Diego • New Haven, Conn.
Waterville, Maine • London • Munich

© 2005 Thomson Gale, a part of The Thomson Corporation.

Thomson and Star Logo are trademarks and Gale and Greenhaven Press are registered trademarks used herein under license.

For more information, contact
Greenhaven Press
27500 Drake Rd.
Farmington Hills, MI 48331-3535
Or you can visit our Internet site at http://www.gale.com

Cover credit: © Ted Horowitz/CORBIS

LIBRARY OF CONGRESS CATALOGING-IN-PUBLICATION DATA

Germs / Beth Donovan Reh, book editor.
    p. cm. — (Exploring science and medical discoveries)
Includes bibliographical references and index.
ISBN 0-7377-2825-6 (lib. bdg.)
    1. Medical microbiology. 2. Bacteria. 3. Infection. 4. Communicable diseases.
5. Germ theory of disease. I. Reh, Beth Donovan. II. Series.
QR46.G455   2005
616.9'041—dc22   2004061692

Printed in the United States of America

CONTENTS

Chapter 2: The War Against Germs

Chapter 3: New Challenges

Chapter 4: Germ Controversies

FOREWORD

Most great science and medical discoveries emerge slowly from the work of generations of scientists. In their laboratories, far removed from the public eye, scientists seek cures for human diseases, explore more efficient methods to feed the world's hungry, and develop technologies to improve quality of life. A scientist, trained in the scientific method, may spend his or her entire career doggedly pursuing a goal such as a cure for cancer or the invention of a new drug. In the pursuit of these goals, most scientists are single-minded, rarely thinking about the moral and ethical issues that might arise once their new ideas come into the public view. Indeed, it could be argued that scientific inquiry requires just that type of objectivity.

Moral and ethical assessments of scientific discoveries are quite often made by the unscientific—the public—sometimes for good, sometimes for ill. When a discovery is unveiled to society, intense scrutiny often ensues. The media report on it, politicians debate how it should be regulated, ethicists analyze its impact on society, authors vilify or glorify it, and the public struggles to determine whether the new development is friend or foe. Even without fully understanding the discovery or its potential impact, the public will often demand that further inquiry be stopped. Despite such negative reactions, however, scientists rarely quit their pursuits; they merely find ways around the roadblocks.

Embryonic stem cell research, for example, illustrates this tension between science and public response. Scientists engage in embryonic stem cell research in an effort to treat diseases such as Parkinson's and diabetes that are the result of cellular dysfunction. Embryonic stem cells can be derived from early-stage embryos, or blastocysts, and coaxed to form any kind of human cell or tissue. These can then be used to replace damaged or diseased tissues in those suffering from intractable diseases. Many researchers believe that the use of embryonic stem cells to treat human diseases promises to be one of the most important advancements in medicine.

However, embryonic stem cell experiments are highly contro-
versial in the public sphere. At the center of the tumult is the fact
that in order to create embryonic stem cell lines, human embryos
must be destroyed. Blastocysts often come from fertilized eggs that
are left over from fertility treatments. Critics argue that since blastocysts have the capacity to grow into human beings, they should
be granted the full range of rights given to all humans, including
the right not to be experimented on. These analysts contend, therefore, that destroying embryos is unethical. This argument received
attention in the highest office of the United States. President
George W. Bush agreed with the critics, and in August 2001 he announced that scientists using federal funds to conduct embryonic
stem cell research would be restricted to using existing cell lines.
He argued that limiting research to existing lines would prevent any
new blastocysts from being destroyed for research.

Scientists have criticized Bush's decision, saying that restrict-
ing research to existing cell lines severely limits the number and
types of experiments that can be conducted. Despite this considerable roadblock, however, scientists quickly set to work trying to
figure out a way to continue their valuable research. Unsurpris-
ingly, as the regulatory environment in the United States becomes
restrictive, advancements occur elsewhere. A good example concerns the latest development in the field. On February 12, 2004,
professor Hwang Yoon-Young of Hanyang University in Seoul,
South Korea, announced that he was the first to clone a human
embryo and then extract embryonic stem cells from it. Hwang's
research means that scientists may no longer need to use blastocysts to perform stem cell research. Scientists around the world
extol the achievement as a major step in treating human diseases.

The debate surrounding embryonic stem cell research illustrates
the moral and ethical pressure that the public brings to bear on the
scientific community. However, while nonexperts often criticize
scientists for not considering the potential negative impact of their
work, ironically the public's reaction against such discoveries can
produce harmful results as well. For example, although the outcry
against embryonic stem cell research in the United States has resulted in fewer embryos being destroyed, those with Parkinson's,
such as actor Michael J. Fox, have argued that prohibiting the development of new stem cell lines ultimately will prevent a timely
cure for the disease that is killing Fox and thousands of others.

Greenhaven Press's Exploring Science and Medical Discover-

ies series explores the public uproar that often follows the disclo-
sure of scientific advances in fields such as stem cell research.
Each anthology traces the history of one major scientific or medical discovery, investigates society's reaction to the breakthrough,
and explores potential new applications and avenues of research.
Primary sources provide readers with eyewitness accounts of crucial moments in the discovery process, and secondary sources offer historical perspectives on the scientific achievement and society's reaction to it. Volumes also contain useful research tools,
including an introductory essay providing important context, and
an annotated table of contents enabling students to quickly locate
selections of interest. A thorough index helps readers locate content easily, a detailed chronology helps students trace the history
of the discovery, and an extensive bibliography guides readers interested in pursuing further research.

Greenhaven Press's Exploring Science and Medical Discoveries series provides readers with inspiring accounts of how generations of scientists made the world's great discoveries possible and
investigates the tremendous impact those innovations have had on
the world.

INTRODUCTION

E verybody has an idea of what germs are. Even a preverbal toddler knows not to touch something when Mommy says, "Yuck! Germs!" Yet, establishing an exact definition is not as straightforward as it might seem. The *Merriam-Webster Dictionary* defines a germ as "a small mass of living substance capable of developing into an organism or one of its parts." Inherent in the term from its French and German roots is the idea of beginning or seed or bud. Implied in the term as it is used in the above case is the idea of dirtiness and disease. Some microbiologists use the terms *microbe* and *germ* interchangeably; but, in general, *germ* has the negative association of disease, whereas *microbe* refers to a small organism that may or may not be pathogenic, or harmful.

The first postulation of disease-causing germs was by Italian physician and poet Girolamo Fracastoro, who published in 1546 that disease resulted from the transmission of invisible contagious seeds or "seminaria." However, since no one could see the seeds, the hypothesis was no better or worse than the ancient Greek physician Hippocrates' assumption that certain influences in one's environment resulted in disease.

The Discovery of Microbes

Therefore, through the sixteenth century, diseases were attributed to miasmas, supernatural retribution, and an imbalance of body humors (blood, phlegm, yellow bile, and black bile). The invention of the microscope in the seventeenth century led scientists to explore the structure of matter, but these first microscopes were not very powerful and observers did not notice microbial creatures. It was not a formal scientist who observed the first microbes. Antoni van Leeuwenhoek was a Dutch dry goods merchant and a janitor, but he was also very curious about the world around him. He made his own lenses to examine textiles, and when he wanted to see more detail, he made more powerful lenses. With these lenses, he constructed microscopes that had better magnification than others used in Europe at that time. Leeuwenhoek used his microscopes to examine many specimens in his environment. When he looked at a sample of rainwater, though, he made his most impressive discovery. He saw little, moving creatures that he called animalcules. Fascinated with the tiny world, he began to examine everything around him, and he found these microscopic creatures on or in everything he investigated.

Over the last half of the seventeenth century, Leeuwenhoek shared his observations with the Royal Society of London, and eminent scientists, such as Robert Hooke, duplicated his experiments. The world of microbes had been found, and there were untold numbers of them living everywhere. Leeuwenhoek commented, "There are more animals living in the scum of the teeth of a man's mouth, than there are men in an entire kingdom."[1]

Neither Leeuwenhoek nor the other observers ever formally entertained the idea that these tiny animalcules could harm a huge person, let alone cause disease and epidemics. It would have been laughable to many of that age to even think of such an idea. In the seventeenth century, Christian Europe was broadening its scientific understanding of the world; however, many still turned to religion for answers and science for mere curiosity. Their religion taught that diseases were a punishment from God and that humans were separate from animals and plants and all the rest of creation. There was no firm idea of the interrelatedness of living things, and there was certainly no idea that something as small as a microbe could affect, in any way, something as large and superior as a human. Tiny animals were interesting to look at, but they could not possibly have any consequence for humans.

The Fight Against Contagious Disease

Whether a punishment from God or an imbalance of humors was the supposed cause of disease, it was all too obvious that certain diseases could spread among populations. There was no understanding of how or why they spread, but somehow, contact made a difference. To reduce exposure communities practiced quarantine and thus separated the obviously sick from the supposedly healthy. Isolation of lepers dates back to the Old Testament, and formal quarantine of ships during epidemics was practiced in Europe since the fourth century. For highly contagious diseases such as plague, people did not need to know about germs to know that contact with a plague-ridden person, dead or alive, could mean death.

Then, in the 1700s some of Europe's scientists and scholars observed that where there was filth, there was more disease. Sensing a relationship, these observers made their views public. The result was the Sanitary Awakening, a period lasting through the 1800s, in which reformers pushed to clean up cities and towns, provide clean water, dispose of waste in certain designated areas, and isolate sick people in hospitals. These efforts led to the decline of many infectious diseases even before any causes were understood.

In the 1840s a similar cause-and-effect observation led one reformer, Hungarian doctor Ignaz Semmelweis, to institute a hand-washing policy for the doctors in his charge. Semmelweis had noticed that women who delivered babies with doctors were more likely to die of puerperal (childbed) fever than those who delivered with midwives. He knew that the doctors often spent their days dealing with the sick and the dead, and therefore any children born on such days might be exposed to unknown contagions. Midwives did not normally contend with the sick, so they were less likely to be transmitters of disease. Semmelweis's predictions proved correct; with hand washing, the incidence of puerperal fever in his hospital dropped dramatically. However, many doctors at the time were offended at the suggestion that their dirty hands might be the cause of a disease. It was one thing to clean up their cities, but no one could require them to wash their hands. In fact, Semmelweis was censured and punished by the medical establishment for challenging the system, even though his policy was saving lives.

Semmelweis did not know exactly why hand washing was important, but he knew that it worked. Many early reformers operated from similar ignorance. They did not understand exactly why filthy cities had more disease than clean towns, but they knew from observation that better sanitation led to improved health in the community. Some nineteenth-century reformers and scientists, however, began making connections between certain microbes and specific diseases. A few even speculated that the microbes might be the cause of the diseases, but they could not prove it. One such reformer was English physician John Snow. He proved in 1854 that a local cholera epidemic could be traced to a single contaminated well; and, by removing access to the water, he stopped the epidemic. He also isolated what would eventually be proven to be the causative bacterium, *Vibrio cholerae*, but he could not prove it as the cause at the time.

Most scientists and reformers were not ready to accept the idea that a bacterium could cause disease. It was not until the subsequent establishment of the germ theory of disease that doctors, scientists, and the general public were able to comprehend the root cause of contagiousness. As this understanding of germs grew, the ability to combat and cure specific diseases flourished.

The Germ Theory of Disease

In the mid-1800s the French chemist Louis Pasteur was the first to postulate that a specific germ caused a specific disease. Pasteur's hypothesis was immediately accepted by some but challenged by others. Yet the more research done to either prove or disprove Pasteur's hypothesis, the more the results supported the germ theory. In 1876 German doctor Robert Koch provided overwhelming proof that a specific bacillus (rod-shaped bacterium) caused the disease anthrax. Further studies by Pasteur supported that conclusion, and the scientific community was forced to accept that bacteria could cause disease in animals.

During his studies Koch outlined a method to establish disease causation that is still used today. Known as Koch's postulates, the system states that in order to prove that a certain microbe causes a disease, one must first isolate the foreign microbe from a diseased individual. The isolated microbe should then be grown in pure culture and inoculated into a healthy individual. When the healthy individual develops the same disease, the same type of organism should be extracted from the newly diseased individual. Koch used this procedure, as well as his new techniques of bacteria staining and growing pure cultures, to demonstrate that the human disease tuberculosis (TB) was caused by a unique type of bacillus. From Koch's techniques the field of microbiology was established. Research institutes sprang up, such as the Pasteur Institute and the Koch Institute, and they brought seasoned and budding scientists together to study germs and disease.

The War on Germs

Almost as soon as Pasteur formed his germ theory, he and others were using it to try to fight disease. Initially, Pasteur recalled Edward Jenner's work with smallpox almost one hundred years earlier. Jenner had observed that milkmaids who had had cowpox infections did not succumb to smallpox. Therefore, he infected people with cowpox to prevent smallpox. Jenner's work influenced Pasteur by suggesting that immunity could be induced through vaccination—the purposeful infection of individuals with a weakened strain of a disease. Pasteur grew cultures of germs and then weakened them to develop vaccines for chicken cholera, anthrax, and rabies. Embolded by his progress, Pasteur stated, "It is in the power of man to make parasitic maladies disappear from the face of the globe."[2]

Following the methods used for anthrax and TB, researchers isolated disease-causing germs one by one and then tried to develop treatments, vaccines, and controls. Some germs, such as TB, proved impossible to develop a vaccine for. Other germs such as those that cause hoof-and-mouth disease and yellow fever were found to be too small to view with a microscope, so their vaccines remained beyond reach until technologies for viewing them and growing them in pure culture were developed. Except for the viruses whose vaccines were developed in total ignorance of the germ being a virus (smallpox and rabies, for example), virus vaccines did not emerge until the second half of the twentieth century.

Still, germs seemed to be losing the war. Vaccines thwarted some. Others were fought by controlling the means by which they spread. Germs such as cholera were identified in drinking water and were controlled by sanitizing water sources. Malaria was traced to mosquitoes, and the disease was contained by destroying mosquito populations. Persons infected with malaria could also be treated with quinine, a chemical made from the bark of the South American cinchona tree.

The idea of chemical cures was just as appealing to many researchers as that of vaccines. In 1912 German physician Paul Ehrlich (working in Koch's laboratory) announced the discovery of an effective cure for syphilis. Thus, salvarsan, or agent 606, became the first specific chemotherapeutic agent for a bacterial disease. Ehrlich brought news of the treatment to London, where Scottish bacteriologist Alexander Fleming became one of the few physicians to advocate the new drug and administer it regularly. In 1928 Fleming discovered that a common soil fungus that had contaminated a culture in his lab was producing something that killed the bacteria he was studying. Knowing salvarsan's power,

Fleming suspected that he had stumbled onto a drug of some value. He called the substance penicillin. Fleming published a paper on the substance and noted that it could be useful if produced in quantity. Then, in 1938 Australian pathologist Howard Florey and German-Jewish biochemist Ernst Chain came across Fleming's paper on penicillin while working in England. Their experiments led to commercially available penicillin by 1942. The wonder drug—one of the earliest antibiotics—saved thousands of lives during World War II and in later decades.

The twentieth century was a time of major change in the field of medicine, especially in relation to infectious disease. In 1900 the leading causes of death in the United States were pneumonia, TB, enteritis, and diphtheria. These diseases accounted for more than one-third of all deaths (40 percent of which were children under five). In 1997 the leading causes of death were heart disease and cancer, which accounted for more than 50 percent of all deaths. Only 4.5 percent of deaths in 1997 were attributed to infectious disease. The decrease in contagion-related deaths was due to the advent of antibiotics that treat bacterial diseases and to other drugs that combat certain viral, fungal, and parasitic infections. At the dawn of the twenty-first century, there are twenty-one vaccine-preventable diseases. Children in the United States are immunized against ten of these by the age of five. Smallpox has been completely eradicated from the world, and death in the United States from at least seven other diseases has been reduced to near zero.

Today researchers can scientifically study detailed cause-effect relationships, and doctors can effectively attack specific germs to cure diseases. All of the discoveries about germs led to aseptic techniques, better personal and community hygiene, preventative vaccination, and chemotherapeutic treatments. They also led to new fields such as molecular genetics and biotechnology, which allowed doctors to understand germs on a subcellular level.

The Resilience of Germs

The golden age of microbiology—which lasted roughly from the 1890s to the 1980s—revolved around attacking germs, but the attacks were executed without an understanding of how microbes interact with and are interrelated to the living world. Many of the microbe hunters, including Louis Pasteur, had the noble goal of ridding the world from infectious disease. However, it took a century to realize that such a goal was naive. While battling one bug, others got stronger because they developed resistance to their antibiotic remedies. Similarly, preventing infection in infants often led to bouts with a disease (such as polio or tuberculosis) later in life once the germs had time to adapt to the preventative measures. This failure to understand microbial evolution was a natural mistake based on the knowledge of the time.

In the late 1800s the scientific world was adjusting to two major paradigm shifts, the evolution of species and the germ theory of disease. These theories needed time to sink into both the scientific and the public mind, and they needed testing. Their general acceptance came slowly to the masses. Even slower was the merging of the ideas from these two theories. It took time and documentation to show that studying the evolutionary process of germs is as important as studying the germs themselves. New generations of germs can evolve in days, and germs can share genetic information with each other, even among different species, without mating. As researchers began to be aware of the intricacies and abilities of microbial evolution, it became clear that trying to eradicate a single species of germ is much harder than wiping out a species of a higher organism.

Germs adapt quickly. They have been in a coevolutionary battle with humans since the dawn of man, and humans have only been consciously involved in this battle since the 1880s. The diseases that were studied and controlled in the twentieth century provided a sense of security. However, diseases once thought to be controlled such as TB, staphylococcus, streptococcus, and pneumococcal infections, are resurfacing in the twenty-first century. Many of these are returning because of antibiotic resistance. By escalating the war on germs and bombarding them with drugs, humans have ignored the fact that through the process of natural selection, strains of germs arise that resist the drugs. Once one germ or virus survives an antibiotic or a disinfectant, that resistance trait can be shared with other strains. As long as the microbes with that trait fare well in the environment, the resistance continues and spreads. Journalist Judith Braffman-Miller took this fact to its natural conclusion when she stated, "As bacteria learn to adapt to drugs that once killed them, mankind could be facing a return to the days when even minor infections could turn deadly for lack of effective treatment."[3]

Other infectious diseases wax and wane naturally each year. It is now known that some germs, such as those that cause influenza, evolve, or change, every season, and new, speculative vaccines must be made each year. Some years the change results in a mild flu bug, and some years a highly virulent strain emerges.

At the same time that old diseases are coming back, new diseases are appearing, such as HIV/AIDS, E. coli gastroenteritis, Legionnaire's disease, Lyme disease, and hantavirus diseases. In addition to these recognizable diseases and their known causes is a potentially new disease agent, the prion. Not a microbe or a virus, the prion is merely a misshaped protein that some researchers believe to be the infectious cause of a number of neurodegenerative spongiform encephalopathies (brain diseases). These newly emerging and reemerging infectious diseases—at least thirty since 1950—remind the world that germs are not so easily controlled and that there is a lot more to learn about them.

Coexistence with Germs

The discovery of the germ theory and the resulting war on germs was a first step toward controlling infectious disease. However, the war itself is evolving based on newer understandings of the interrelatedness of all living things and of microbial evolution. It is now common knowledge that not all microorganisms are disease-causing germs and that microorganisms have interactive functions with most living and nonliving things. It is also well known that microbes share genetic information easily, evolve quickly, and are more likely to adapt than die out. There will always be microbes in this world, and therefore, there will always be germs. They were here long before humans, and they will probably still be here when the earth is no longer habitable by humans. As Nicholas Bakalar states in the introduction to his book *Where the Germs Are*, "Sometimes you read of the 'age of dinosaurs' or 'the age of reptiles' or hear people speak of the time we live in now as 'the age of mammals.' But in fact, we are in—and always have been in since the beginning of life on earth—the age of microbes."[4] Microbes inhabit all parts of the world, and they are tied into the global ecology in ways that humans cannot presume to fully understand yet. Some scientists argue that humans should no longer be so arrogant as to believe that it is possible to eliminate all germs. In 1976 William H. McNeill, professor emeritus of history at the University of Chicago, wrote in his book *Plagues and Peo-*

ples, "Ingenuity, knowledge, and organization alter but cannot cancel humanity's vulnerability to invasion by parasitic forms of life. Infectious disease which antedated the emergence of humankind will last as long as humanity itself, and will surely remain, as it has been hitherto, one of the fundamental parameters and determinants of human history."[5]

For these researchers who recognize the adaptability of germs, the time has come to shift away from the war metaphor. Controlling, or even eliminating if possible, the very worst radical killers (such as smallpox or tuberculosis) is still a priority, but there is now an emphasis on coexisting with the less deadly germs and allowing the beneficial microbes to keep those germs in check. Since germs and humans have coevolved, the ecological niche of germs involves humans, and the ecological niche of humans involves germs. Understanding this coexistence may be humanity's best means of controlling the most virulent germs without upsetting the balance of nature that keeps people and microbes alive.

Notes

1. Quoted in Tonse N.K. Raju, "A Most Improbable Scientist," *Hippocrates*, January 2001.
2. Quoted in Robert DeSalle, ed., *Epidemic! The World of Infectious Disease*. New York: New Press, 1999, p. 1.
3. Judith Braffman-Miller, "Beware the Rise of Antibiotic-Resistant Microbes," *USA Today*, March 1997.
4. Nicholas Bakalar, *Where the Germs Are*. Hoboken, NJ: John Wiley, 2003, p. 7.
5. William H. McNeill, *Plagues and Peoples*. New York: Doubleday, 1976, p. 257.

CHAPTER 1

The Discovery of Germs

Leeuwenhoek's Wretched Beasties

By Paul de Kruif

Paul de Kruif was a trained biologist who turned to writing. His most notable work is *Microbe Hunters*. Published in 1926, it is still in print today. In the first chapter, which is excerpted below, de Kruif introduces Antoni van Leeuwenhoek, the first of the microbe hunters. Though not a trained scientist, Leeuwenhoek was keenly interested in the world around him. He ground his own lenses and made his own microscopes so that he could observe anything and everything in minute detail. His lenses were more powerful than any in Europe at the time, and his observations astounded the Royal Society of London. When he wrote to that renown organization of his observation of "wretched beasties" in samples of rainwater, the society had esteemed scientist Robert Hooke duplicate Leeuwenhoek's work so they too could view the previously unseen microbial world. Leeuwenhoek sent letters to the Royal Society for the next fifty years that documented his ongoing examination of the tiny life-forms that seemed to be present on everything that went under his microscope.

[I n the mid-1600s] an obscure man named Leeuwenhoek looked for the first time into a mysterious new world peopled with a thousand different kinds of tiny beings, some ferocious and deadly, others friendly and useful, many of them more important to mankind than any continent or archipelago.

Leeuwenhoek, unsung and scarce remembered, is now almost as unknown as his strange little animals and plants were at the time he discovered them. This is the story of Leeuwenhoek, the first of the microbe hunters. . . .

Take yourself back to Leeuwenhoek's day . . . and imagine

Paul de Kruif, *Microbe Hunters*. New York: Harcourt, Brace and Company, 1926.

yourself just through high school, getting ready to choose a career, wanting to know—

You have lately recovered from an attack of mumps, you ask your father what is the cause of mumps and he tells you a mumpish evil spirit has got into you. His theory may not impress you much, but you decide to make believe you believe him and not to wonder any more about what is mumps—because if you publicly don't believe him you are in for a beating and may even be turned out of the house. Your father is Authority.

That was the world . . . when Leeuwenhoek was born. It had hardly begun to shake itself free from superstitions, it was barely beginning to blush for its ignorance. It was a world where science (which only means trying to find truth by careful observation and clear thinking) was just learning to toddle on vague and wobbly legs. It was a world where Servetus was burned to death for daring to cut up and examine the body of a dead man, where Galileo was shut up for life for daring to prove that the earth moved around the sun.

Merchant, Janitor, Lens-Grinder

Antony Leeuwenhoek was born in 1632 . . . in Holland. . . . He left school at sixteen to be an apprentice in a dry-goods store in Amsterdam. That was his university. Think of a present-day scientist getting his training for experiment among bolts of gingham, listening to the tinkle of the bell on the cash drawer, being polite to an eternal succession of Dutch housewives who shopped with a penny-pinching dreadful exhaustiveness—but that was Leeuwenhoek's university, for six years!

At the age of twenty-one he left the dry-goods store, went back to Delft, married, set up a dry-goods store of his own there. For twenty years after that very little is known about him, except that he had two wives (in succession) and several children most of whom died, but there is no doubt that during this time he was appointed janitor of the city hall of Delft, and that he developed a most idiotic love for grinding lenses. He had heard that if you very carefully ground very little lenses out of clear glass, you would see things look much bigger than they appeared to the naked eye. . . . Little is known about him from twenty to forty, but there is no doubt that he passed in those days for an ignorant man. The only language he knew was Dutch—that was an obscure language despised by the cultured world as a tongue of fishermen and shop-keepers and diggers of ditches. Educated men talked Latin in those days, but Leeuwenhoek could not so much as read it and his only literature was the Dutch Bible. Just the same, you will see that his ignorance was a great help to him, for, cut off from all of the learned nonsense of his time, he had to trust his own eyes, his own thoughts, his own judgment. . . .

During these twenty years of his obscurity he went to spectacle-makers and got the rudiments of lens-grinding. He visited al-chemists and apothecaries and put his nose into their secret ways of setting metals from ores, he began fumblingly to learn the craft of the gold- and silversmiths. He was a most pernickety man and was not satisfied with grinding lenses as good as those of the best lens-grinder in Holland, they had to be better than the best, and then he still fussed over them for long hours. Next he mounted these lenses in little oblongs of copper or silver or gold, which he had ex-tracted himself, over hot fires, among strange smells and fumes. . . .

Now this self-satisfied dry-goods dealer began to turn his lenses onto everything he could get hold of. He looked through them at the muscle fibers of a whale and the scales of his own skin. He went to the butcher shop and begged or bought ox-eyes and was amazed at how prettily the crystalline lens of the eye of the ox is put together. He peered for hours at the build of the hairs of a sheep, of a beaver, of an elk, that were transformed from their fine-ness into great rough logs under his bit of glass. He delicately dis-sected the head of a fly; he stuck its brain on the fine needle of his microscope—how he admired the clear details of the marvelous big brain of that fly! He examined the cross-sections of the wood of a dozen different trees and squinted at the seeds of plants. He grunted "Impossible!" when he first spied the outlandish large per-fection of the sting of a flea and the legs of a louse. . . .

Fastidious Observer

There never was a less sure man than Leeuwenhoek. He looked at this bee's sting or that louse's leg again and again and again. He left his specimens sticking on the point of his strange microscope for months—in order to look at other things he made more mi-croscopes till he had hundreds of them!—then he came back to those first specimens to correct his first mistakes. He never set down a word about anything he peeped at, he never made a drawing until hundreds of peeps showed him that, under given conditions, he would always see exactly the same thing. And then he was not sure! He said:

"People who look for the first time through a microscope say now I see this and then I see that—and even a skilled observer can be fooled. On these observations I have spent more time than many will believe, but I have done them with joy, and I have taken no notice of those who have said why take so much trouble and what good is it?—but I do not write for such people but only for the philosophical!" He worked for twenty years that way, without an audience.

But at this time, in the middle of the seventeenth century, great things were astir in the world. Here and there in France and England and Italy rare men were thumbing their noses at almost everything that passed for knowledge. "We will no longer take Aristotle's say-so, nor the Pope's say-so," said these rebels. "We will trust only the perpetually repeated observations of our own eyes and the careful weighings of our scales; we will listen to the answers experiments give us and no other answers!" So in England a few of these revolutionists started a society called The Invisible College, it had to be invisible because that man [British ruler Oliver] Cromwell might have hung them for plotters and heretics if he had heard of the strange questions they were trying to settle. . . .

When Charles II came to the throne, it rose from its depths as a sort of blind-pig scientific society to the dignity of the name of the Royal Society of England. And they were Antony Leeuwenhoek's first audience! There was one man in Delft who did not laugh at Antony Leeuwenhoek, and that was Regnier de Graaf, whom the Lords and Gentlemen of the Royal Society had made a corresponding member because he had written them of interesting things he had found in the human ovary. Already Leeuwenhoek was rather surly and suspected everybody, but he let de Graaf peep through those magic eyes of his, those little lenses whose equal did not exist in Europe or England or the whole world for that matter. What de Graaf saw through those microscopes made him ashamed of his own fame and he hurried to write to the Royal Society:

"Get Antony Leeuwenhoek to write you telling of his discoveries."

And Leeuwenhoek answered the request of the Royal Society with all the confidence of an ignorant man who fails to realize the profound wisdom of the philosophers he addresses. It was a long letter, it rambled over every subject under the sun, it was written with a comical artlessness in the conversational Dutch that was the only language he knew. The title of that letter was: "A Specimen of some Observations made by a Microscope contrived by Mr. Leeuwenhoek, concerning Mould upon the Skin, Flesh, etc.; the Sting of a Bee, etc." The Royal Society was amazed, the sophisticated and learned gentlemen were amused—but principally the Royal Society was astounded by the marvelous things Leeuwenhoek told them he could see through his new lenses. The Secretary of the Royal Society thanked Leeuwenhoek and told him he hoped his first communication would be followed by others. It was, by hundreds of others over a period of fifty years. . . .

Little Animals

Yes, and all this squinting at bee-stings and mustache hairs and what-not were needful to prepare him for that sudden day when he looked through his toy of a gold-mounted lens at a fraction of a small drop of clear rain water to discover—

What he saw that day starts this history. Leeuwenhoek was a maniac observer, and who but such a strange man would have thought to turn his lens on clear, pure water, just come down from the sky? What could there be in water but just—water? You can imagine his daughter Maria—she was nineteen and she took such care of her slightly insane father!—watching him take a little tube of glass, heat it red-hot in a flame, draw it out to the thinness of a hair. . . . Maria was devoted to her father—let any of those stupid neighbors dare to snigger at him!—but what in the world was he up to now, with that hairfine glass pipe? . . .

Then suddenly the excited voice of Leeuwenhoek: "Come here! Hurry! There are little animals in the rain water. . . . They swim. They play around. They are a thousand times smaller than any creatures we can see with our eyes alone. . . . Look! See what I have discovered!" . . .

How marvelous it would be to step into that simple Dutchman's shoes, to be inside his brain and body, to feel his excitement—it is almost nausea!—at his first peep at those cavorting "wretched beasties."

That was what he called them, and, as I have told you, this Leeuwenhoek was an unsure man. Those animals were too tremendously small to be true, they were too strange to be true. So he looked again, till his hands were cramped with holding his microscope and his eyes full of that smarting water that comes from too-long looking. But he was right! Here they were again, not one kind of little creature, but here was another, larger than the first, "moving about very nimbly because they were furnished with divers incredibly thin feet." Wait! Here is a third kind—and a fourth, so tiny I can't make out his shape. But he is alive! He goes about, dashing over great distances in this world of his water-drop in the little tube. . . . What nimble creatures!

"They stop, they stand still as 'twere upon a point, and then turn themselves round with that swiftness, as we see a top turn round, the circumference they make being no bigger than that of a fine grain of sand." So wrote Leeuwenhoek.

For all this seemingly impractical snipping about, Leeuwenhoek was a hard-headed man. He hardly ever spun theories, he was a friend for measuring things. Only how could you make a measuring stick for anything so small as these little beasts? He wrinkled his low forehead: "How large really is this last and smallest of the little beasts?" He poked about in the cobwebbed corners of his memory among the thousand other things he had studied with you can't imagine what thoroughness; he made calculations: "This last kind of animal is a thousand times smaller than the eye of a large louse!" That was an accurate man. For we know now that the eye of one fullgrown louse is no larger nor smaller than the eyes of ten thousand of his brother and sister lice.

But where did these outlandish little inhabitants of the rainwater come from? . . .

Experiments

He washed out a wine glass very clean, he dried it, he held it under the spout of his eaves-trough, he took a wee drop in one of his hair-fine tubes. Under his lens it went. . . . Yes! They were there, a few of those beasts, swimming about. . . . "They are present even in very fresh rain water!" But then, that really proved nothing, they might live in the eaves-trough and be washed down by the water. . . .

Then he took a big porcelain dish, "glazed blue within," he washed it clean, out into the rain he went with it and put it on top of a big box so that the falling raindrops would splash no mud into the dish. The first water he threw out to clean it still more thor-

oughly. Then intently he collected the next bit in one of his slen-
der pipes, into his study he went with it. . . .

"I have proved it! This water has not a single little creature in
it! They do not come down from the sky!" But he kept that water;
hour after hour, day after day he squinted at it—and on the fourth
day he saw those wee beasts beginning to appear in the water
along with bits of dust and little flecks of thread and lint. . . .

Did he write to the Royal Society to tell them of this entirely
unsuspected world of life he had discovered? Not yet! He was a
slow man. He turned his lens onto all kinds of water. . . .

His new beasties were marvelous but they were not enough for
him, he was always poking into everything, trying to see more
closely, trying to find reasons. Why is the sharp taste of pepper?
That was what he asked himself one day, and he guessed: "There
must be little points on the particles of pepper and these points jab
the tongue when you eat pepper. . . ."

But are there such little points?

He fussed with dry pepper. He sneezed. He sweat, but he couldn't
set the grains of pepper small enough to put under his lens. So, to
soften it, he put it to soak for several weeks in water. Then with
fine needles he pried the almost invisible specks of the pepper
apart, and sucked them up in a little drop of water into one of his
hair fine glass tubes. He looked—

Here was something to make even this determined man scatter-
brained. He forgot about possible small sharp points on the pepper.
With the interest of an intent little boy he watched the antics of "an
incredible number of little animals, of various sorts, which move
very prettily, which tumble about and sidewise, this way and that!"

So it was Leeuwenhoek stumbled on a magnificent way to grow
his new little animals.

Sharing the Discovery

And now to write all this to the great men off there in London!
Artlessly he described his own astonishment to them. Long page
after page in a superbly neat handwriting with little common
words he told them that you could put a million of these little animals into a coarse grain of sand and that one drop of his pepper-
water, where they grew and multiplied so well, held more than
two-million seven-hundred-thousand of them. . . .

This letter was translated into English. It was read before the learned skeptics—who no longer believed in the magic virtues of unicorn's horns—and it bowled the learned body over! What! The Dutchman said he had discovered beasts so small that you could put as many of them into one little drop of water as there were people in his native country? Nonsense! The cheese-mite was absolutely and without doubt the smallest creature God had created.

But a few of the members did not scoff. This Leeuwenhoek was a confoundedly accurate man: everything he had ever written to them they had found to be true. . . . So a letter went back to the scientific janitor, begging him to write them in detail the way he had made his microscope, and his method of observing. . . .

Years of Observation and Documentation

Those little animals were everywhere! He told the Royal Society of finding swarms of those sub-visible beings in his mouth—of all places: "Although I am now fifty years old," he wrote, "I have uncommonly well-preserved teeth, because it is my custom every morning to rub my teeth very hard with salt, and after cleaning my large teeth with a quill, to rub them vigorously with a cloth. . . ." But there still were little bits of white stuff between his teeth, when he looked at them with a magnifying mirror. . . .

What was this white stuff made of?

From his teeth he scraped a bit of this stuff, mixed it with pure rain water, stuck it in a little tube on to the needle of his microscope, closed the door of his study—

What was this that rose from the gray dimness of his lens into clear distinctness as he brought the tube into the focus? Here was an unbelievably tiny creature, leaping about in the water of the tube "like the fish called a pike." There was a second kind that swam forward a little way, then whirled about suddenly, then tumbled over itself in pretty somersaults. There were some beings that moved sluggishly and looked like wee bent sticks, nothing more, but that Dutchman squinted at them till his eyes were red-rimmed—and they moved, they were alive, no doubt of it! There was a menagerie in his mouth! There were creatures shaped like flexible rods that went to and fro with the stately carriage of bishops in procession, there were spirals that whirled through the water like violently animated corkscrews. . . .

You may wonder that Leeuwenhoek nowhere in any of those hundreds of letters makes any mention of the harm these mysterious new little animals might do to men. He had come upon them in drinking water, spied upon them in the mouth; as the years went by he discovered them in the intestines of frogs and horses, and even in his own discharges; in swarms he found them on those rare occasions when, as he says, "he was troubled with a looseness." But not for a moment did he guess that his trouble was caused by those little beasts, and from his unimaginativeness and his carefulness not to jump to conclusions modern microbe hunters—if they only had time to study his writings—could learn a great deal. For, during the last fifty years, literally thousands of microbes have been described as the authors of hundreds of diseases, when, in the majority of cases those germs have only been chance residents in the body at the time it became diseased. Leeuwenhoek was cautious about calling anything the *cause* of anything else. He had a sound instinct about the infinite complicatedness of everything— that told him the danger of trying to pick out one cause from the tangled maze of causes which control life.

Establishing the Germ Theory of Disease

By René J. Dubos

René J. Dubos was a microbiologist whose research led to the discovery and production of many antibiotics. He was also a Pulitzer Prize–winning author and an environmentalist who influenced the way in which many modern scientists view the interrelatedness of all life. He coined the well-known phrase, "Think globally, act locally." His many writings merge his microbial training with his environmental and social philosophies. In the following selection from his 1950 biography of French scientist Louis Pasteur, Dubos explains the evolution and acceptance of the germ theory of disease in the late 1800s. Pasteur's studies on fermentation and putrefaction and his experiments to disprove the theory of spontaneous generation of life led him to conclude that germs must be the cause of infectious disease. Scottish doctor Joseph Lister believed Pasteur's hypothesis and developed aseptic techniques for surgery and hospitals, which resulted in an enormous drop in the number of infections. This success and many experiments by Pasteur and other scientists demonstrated support for his germ hypothesis. Still, many other scientists were skeptical. Then, a country doctor, Robert Koch, published his studies on anthrax and demonstrated irrefutably that one specific type of bacillus (rod-shaped bacteria) was indeed the cause of anthrax. Pasteur performed his own experiments on anthrax which supported Koch's findings. The germ theory of disease was proven, and the study of infectious disease was revolutionized.

There is no doubt that Pasteur's demonstration, between 1857 and 1876, that the "infinitely small" play an "infinitely great role" in the economy of matter prepared the medical mind

René J. Dubos, *Louis Pasteur: Free Lance of Science*. Boston: Little, Brown and Company, 1950.

to recognize that microorganisms can behave as agents of disease. The proof that fermentation and putrefaction were caused by fungi, yeasts and bacteria revealed a number of relationships which had their counterparts in the phenomena of contagion [i.e., the spread of disease]. It established that the effects of microorganisms could be entirely out of proportion to their size and mass and that they exhibited a remarkable specificity, each microbial type being adapted to the performance of a limited set of biochemical reactions. The microorganisms carried out these reactions as a result of their living processes, they increased in number during the course of the reaction, and thus could be transferred endlessly to new media and induce again the alterations over which they presided. . . .

Pasteur's . . . demonstration that different types of living germs are widely distributed in the atmosphere gave a concrete basis to the vague view that agents of disease could be transmitted through the air. Pasteur himself had repeatedly emphasized this possible consequence of his findings, but it was the work of Joseph Lister which first established the medical significance of his teaching. . . .

Joseph Lister Considers Germs in Wounds

Lister was a young surgeon in Glasgow when the impact of Pasteur's studies on the distribution of bacteria in the air convinced him of the role of microorganisms in the varied forms of "putric intoxications" which so commonly followed wounds and surgical interventions. Around 1864, he developed the use of antiseptic techniques in surgery with the object of destroying the microorganisms that he assumed to be responsible for the suppurative processes. Lister's methods, at first criticized and ridiculed—particularly in England—were progressively accepted, and became a powerful factor in transferring the germ theory from the experimental domain to the atmosphere of the clinic. In a most generous manner Lister often acknowledged publicly his intellectual debt to Pasteur.

In the introduction to his classical paper "On the Antiseptic Principle in the Practice of Surgery": "When it had been shown by the researches of Pasteur that the septic property of the atmosphere depended, not on the oxygen or a gaseous constituent, but on minute organisms suspended in it, which owed their energy to their vitality, it occurred to me that decomposition in the injured part [i.e., an infected or injured limb] might be avoided without excluding the air, by applying as a dressing some material capable of destroying the life of the floating particles.". . .

Searching for Proof of a Causal Connection

By 1875, the association of microorganisms with disease had received fairly wide acceptance in the medical world. Bacteria had been seen in many types of putrid wounds and other infections. . . . But the mere demonstration that bacteria are present during disease was not proof that they were the cause of it. . . . There were still physicians who believed that microorganisms could organize themselves *de novo* . . . out of diseased tissue. . . . For them, bacterial invasion was only an accidental and secondary consequence of disease, which at best might modify and aggravate the symptoms and pathological changes, but could not be a primary cause. . . .

Despite the official and popular hostility to the germ theory, several physicians and veterinarians attempted to prove between 1860 and 1876 that bacteria could by themselves initiate disease in a healthy body. Pasteur followed these efforts with eagerness . . . and resolutely decided that he too would attack the problem of *anthrax.*" This was in 1876. Unknown to him, a young German country doctor, Robert Koch, had embarked on the same venture the year before; and on April 30, 1876, had presented to Ferdinand Cohn, in the Botanical Institute in Breslau, the complete life history of the anthrax bacillus.

Robert Koch Provides Proof

Koch had frequent occasion to observe anthrax in farm animals in the course of his medical duties. Working in a primitive laboratory that he built in his own home, he established the fact that the disease was transmissible from mouse to mouse and produced typical and reproducible lesions in each member of the successive series of mice. He had also the original idea of placing minute particles of spleens freshly removed from infected animals in drops of sterile blood serum or of aqueous humor, and he began to watch, hour after hour, what took place. His technique was simplicity itself, his apparatus homemade. After twenty hours he saw the anthrax rods grow into long filaments, especially at the edge of the cover glass; and, as he watched, he saw round and oval granular bodies appear in the filaments. He realized that they were spores, similar to those described by Ferdinand Cohn in other bacteria; and he recognized that his cultures underwent a cycle including every stage, from . . . motionless rod to the fully formed spore. He determined the optimal thermal conditions for spore formation and saw that the spores could again grow into typical anthrax rods. Recognizing that the spores were highly resistant to injurious influences, he grasped at once the significance of this property for the maintenance and spread of infection. He learned to differentiate true anthrax from the septicemic disease which had confused the observation of [other scientists]. He further established that the hay bacillus (*Bacillus subtilis*, commonly found in hay infusion), an organism very similar to [the anthrax] rod, and like it capable of producing spores, did not cause anthrax when injected into animals. From all these facts he finally concluded that true anthrax was always induced by only one specific kind of bacillus and he formulated on the basis of this conclusion a number of prophylactic measures aimed at preventing the spread of the disease.

One of Koch's experiments was of particular interest in proving the etiological role of [the anthrax] rods. He had sown fragments of infected tissues into drops of serum or of aqueous humor of the rabbit, and had allowed this primitive culture to incubate until the bacilli had multiplied to large numbers; then, from this first culture, he had inoculated a new drop of serum. After repeating the process eight times he found to his great satisfaction that the last culture injected into a susceptible healthy mouse was as capable of producing anthrax as blood taken directly from an animal just dead of the disease. Despite their thoroughness and elegance, these experiments still left a loophole for those who believed that there was in the blood something besides the rods, capable of inducing anthrax. Although Koch had transferred his cultures eight times in succession, this was not sufficient to rule out the possibility that some hypothetical component of the blood had been carried over from the original drop and was responsible, instead of the bacteria, for transmitting the infection to the inoculated animal. It was this last debatable point that Pasteur's experiments were designed to settle.

Pasteur Enhances Koch's Proof

Pasteur knew from his earlier studies on spontaneous generation that the blood of a healthy animal, taken aseptically during life, and added to any kind of nutrient fluid, would not putrefy or give rise to any living microorganism. He felt confident, therefore, that the blood of an anthrax animal handled with aseptic precautions should give cultures containing only the anthrax bacillus. Experiment soon showed this to be the case, and showed also that rapid and abundant growth of the bacillus could be obtained by cultivating it in neutral urine; these cultures could be readily maintained through countless generations by transfers in the same medium. By adding one drop of blood to fifty cubic centimeters (nearly two ounces) of sterile urine, then, after incubation and multiplication of the bacilli, transferring one drop of this culture into a new flask containing fifty cubic centimeters of urine, and repeating this process one hundred times in succession, Pasteur arrived at a culture in which the dilution of the original blood was so great—of the order of 1 part in 100^{100}—that not even one molecule of it was left in the final material. Only the bacteria could escape the dilution, because they continued to multiply with each transfer. And yet, a drop of the hundredth culture killed a guinea pig, or a rabbit as rapidly as a drop of the original infected blood, thus demonstrating that the "virulence principle" rested in the bacterium, or was produced by it.

Pasteur devised many other ingenious experiments to secure additional evidence of the etiological role of the anthrax bacillus. He filtered cultures through membranes fine enough to hold back the bacteria and showed that the clear filtrate injected into a rabbit did not make it sick. He allowed flasks of culture to rest undisturbed in places of low and constant temperature, until the bacteria had settled to the bottom; again the clear supernatant fluid was found incapable of establishing the disease in experimental animals, whereas a drop of the deposit, containing the bacterial bodies, killed them with anthrax. These results constituted the strongest possible evidence that the anthrax bacillus itself was responsible for the infection. However, Pasteur took care to point out that there still remained a possibility which had not been explored, namely that the bacilli produced a virus which remained associated with them throughout the culture, and which was the active infective agent. But even this hypothesis did not change the conclusion that the bacilli were living and were the cause of anthrax. The germ theory of disease was now firmly established.

Using Pure Cultures to Study Microbes

By Thomas D. Brock

Early in his career, microbiologist Thomas D. Brock published *Milestones in Microbiology*, and, then in the 1970s, he began to focus on the history of microbiology, which yielded, among other writings, a biography of German scientist Robert Koch. This biography, which is excerpted below, was the first one written in English and provides a detailed history infused with many of Koch's original letters and writings. As one of the fathers of bacteriology, Koch contributed much to the field. However, his most significant contributions were not about specific bacteria, but about the techniques necessary for objective, reproducible experiments. One such technique was to grow pure cultures of individual microbial species. The use of pure cultures revolutionized the field of bacteriology and the study of infectious diseases, and it is still practiced today.

Perhaps Koch's greatest contribution to the development of bacteriology and microbiology as independent sciences was his introduction of a pure culture technique using solid or semi-solid media—soon known throughout the world as "Koch's plate technique".

The Pure Culture Technique Before Koch

Pure cultures in the sense we know them today were not obtained by Louis Pasteur or members of his school. Pasteur grew bacteria in transparent liquid media. When growth was evidenced by the development of turbidity in the culture tube, a minute quantity of the culture was inoculated into a fresh medium, and so on in series. By means of serial transfer, Pasteur assumed that a "pure" culture of one type of microorganism would ultimately result. Purity was ascertained primarily by microscopical examination. It was possible in many cases to select a medium that was the most appropriate for a single type of organism and hence obtain some degree of "purity". However, if pure culture was obtained with such procedures, it was just fortuitous. Pasteur's cultures were equivalent to what today would be called "enrichment cultures".

Joseph Lister was the first to obtain a pure culture in liquid medium using a limiting dilution method. Lister's work, published in 1878, was motivated by his desire to show that a single type of bacterium was responsible for a single disease entity. However, rather than studying an infectious disease, he studied the souring of milk by the bacterium that he called *Bacterium lactis*. . . .

More important than Lister's method, however, was his clear enunciation of the *importance* of pure cultures for studies in pathology.

Since Lister was one of Koch's champions in England (it was Lister who had arranged for the English translation of Koch's 1878 book), Koch was certainly aware of Lister's work. He was also aware of the importance of the pure culture for studies on infectious disease. However, until he went to Berlin, methods for obtaining pure cultures in a consistent and reproducible manner eluded him.

A New Technique

One of the first tasks he set himself in his new position was the perfection of all the methods needed for studying pathogenic microorganisms. It is not accidental that the first paper in the first volume of contributions from the Imperial Health Office is Koch's paper on methods for studying pathogens. If one were to choose a single paper as most significant for the rise of microbiology, this would be it. Koch presents a method for isolating pure cultures that is so simple, reproducible, and understandable that it can be performed by almost anyone. During the two decades following its publication, the development of this method led to the isolation and characterization of the causal organisms of almost all of the major bacterial diseases which affected humans.

Background of the Plate Technique

The basis of the plate technique is the development of isolated colonies on solid or semi-solid surfaces. The development of pigmented colonies on the cut surfaces of incubated potatoes was first reported in Breslau in 1875 by Joseph Schroeter (1835–1894), a student of [German botanist] Ferdinand Cohn's. Schroeter studied organisms, . . . pointing out that the color of the pigment was a constant characteristic of the bacterium. He observed that pigment was formed only when the bacterium was growing on the surface of a nutrient substance and concluded that air was necessary for pigment formation. He did a number of studies on the effects of environmental conditions on pigment formation and did simple extraction studies to obtain some idea of the chemistry of the pigments. But the importance of Schroeter's work rested on his single observation that each organism formed a characteristic pigment and that the ability to form this pigment remained upon transfer to a new medium. Schroeter used not only potatoes, but solid media made from starch paste, egg albumin, bread, and meat. It is clear from reading Schroeter's paper that he definitely obtained pure cultures of a wide variety of pigmented bacteria. Koch, a frequent visitor to Cohn's laboratory, was certainly familiar with Schroeter's work, although he does not cite it.

Another important predecessor of Koch was Oscar Brefeld (1839–1925), a German mycologist who made many important contributions to the understanding of the fungi. In 1875, Brefeld laid down precisely the principles which must be followed for obtaining pure cultures. These principles were:

1. The inoculation of the medium should be made from a single fungal spore.

2. The medium should be clear and transparent and should yield optimal growth of the organism.

3. The culture should be kept completely protected from external contamination throughout its existence.

Brefeld's method of inoculating a medium with a single spore was completely for the study of large microorganisms such as fungi but was less useful with the much smaller bacteria. However, his writings had wide influence on the bacteriologists of the day, and Koch certainly built his technique around Brefeld's principles.

The paper which Koch published in 1881 . . . on methods for the study of pathogenic organisms became the "Bible of Bacteriology." The paper not only includes the major section on pure cultures to be discussed here, but also an extensive section on photomicroscopy of bacteria, with the first published photomicrographs of bacteria in diseased tissues. . . .

Koch began the section on pure cultures with this solidly based statement:

> The pure culture is the foundation for all research on infectious diseases.

He then continued:

> The most important procedures that have been developed for the manipulation of pure cultures can be summarized as follows.
>
> A sterilized container is used which has been closed with mold-proof sterilized cotton, and this is filled with a sterilized nutrient liquid of the proper sort. Then this is inoculated with material containing the microorganism which is wanted in pure culture. After reasonable growth has taken place, a sterile instrument is used to transfer a little of this to a second container. This process may be repeated a number of times. . . .
>
> Naturally in this procedure one has to make several assumptions, of which the first is that the culture vessel is really sterile. . . . Even a slight contamination of the inoculum with another species which is faster growing than the organism desired will prevent anyone from ever obtaining a pure culture. . . . All in all, the present situation with regard to pure culture techniques is quite disappointing. Anyone who has cultured microorganisms in the ways currently in vogue will have found how difficult it is to avoid completely all of the sources of error that I have indicated. No one following current methods can complain if his results are not accepted as fact by his fellow workers. What has been said above should be heeded by the Pasteur school in its noteworthy but blindly zealous researchers, since this renders it doubtful that they have obtained in pure culture the organisms of rabies, sheep pox, tuberculosis, and so forth. . . .
>
> The present methods seem to me to offer no hope for a significant improvement. . . . Therefore, I have rejected completely all of the current principles of pure culture and have adopted an entirely new way.

A forthright statement, indeed! In his paper, Koch then turned to an explanation of the rationale for the plate technique that he had developed. . . .

[He then] discusses the kinds of media which pathogenic bacteria can grow on, such as nutrient broths and boullions. Instead of trying to find a solid medium which would support pathogens, he *took a medium which supported the growth of pathogens and made it solid*, by adding gelatin. . . .

> I have carried pathogenic and nonpathogenic organisms over a long series of transfers on boiled potato or nutrient gelatin, without ever once observing any noticeable changes in their characteristics. They maintain their morphological as well as their physiological characteristics . . . without change through months of growth as pure cultures.

It is easy to see how this paper of Koch's became the "Bible of Bacteriology". In a few pages, Koch laid out clearly the essential problem of bacteriological research and provided a solution—a solution so general and widely applicable that it changed for all time the field of bacteriology. Realizing the importance of obtaining pure cultures, Koch took Schroeter's simple observation of the growth of bacterial colonies on potato slices and adapted it to the field of medical bacteriology. The initial challenge arose because many of the pathogenic bacteria Koch was interested in would not grow on potatoes but would grow on nutrient broth media. The solution, therefore, was to convert the nutrient broth into a solid medium. Once the value of this approach had been realized, the whole procedure was generalized. Then it could be applied not only to the growth of pathogenic bacteria but to all kinds of microorganisms. Koch's work described in this paper was an amazing tour de force, one rarely duplicated in the scientific world.

Early Uses of the Plate Technique

Koch realized immediately that the plate technique had many uses besides its value for the isolation of pure culture. Most important, the technique could be used to assess the numbers and kinds of microorganisms found in various environmental samples, such as air, water, soil, food, manufactured objects, etc.

The importance of such studies was enormous. Not only was

the assessment of the microbial content of environmental samples important for public health research, it aided greatly in the improvement of bacteriological technique. Once a quantitative understanding of the microbial populations of habitats such as air and water could be obtained, the development of improved techniques for the laboratory study of microbes became much easier.

Koch was quick to communicate his methods to others. He set up demonstrations in the laboratories of the Imperial Health Office and details of such demonstrations were published in widely available journals.

The Introduction of Agar

Nutrient gelatin was a marvellous culture medium for isolation and study of pure cultures of bacteria, but it had several drawbacks. The most important drawback is that gelatin does not remain solid at body temperature. Thus, one had to incubate cultures at temperatures below their growth optima. In initial studies, this presented no major obstacle, and there are certainly few human pathogens that will not grow at all at room temperature. However, for detailed studies, and for incubation during the summer when room temperature was too high for gelatin to remain solid (these were the days before refrigeration and air conditioning), something better was needed. This "something" was agar (or agar-agar, as it was called in those days).

Agar is a polysaccharide derived from seaweeds of the Rhodophyta. It was used widely in the 19th century, especially in tropical countries, as a gelling agent and had found its way into Europe via trade of the European countries with their tropical colonies. The first use of agar as a solidfying agent for bacteriological culture media was made by Walther Hesse (1846–1911), an associate of Koch's. . . .

Walther Hesse was a physician who worked for half a year in 1881/82 in Koch's laboratory, carrying out quantitative studies on the microorganisms which were found in air . . . in order to learn the new discipline of bacteriology. . . . The actual suggestion to use agar instead of gelatin was made by Hesse's wife, Fannie Eilshemius Hesse, who was not only Hesse's wife but also his technician and artist illustrator. . . .

The counting of bacteria in the air was done by Hesse using a special apparatus that sucked air through tubes lined with gelatin, and the microbial content was assessed by incubating the tubes and counting the colonies which developed. However, in the summer, the gelatin melted during incubation, ruining many experiments. Hesse thus decided to seek a new solidifying agent. Fannie Hesse had used agar for years in the preparation of fruit jellies, following a recipe which she had received from her mother who had in turn learned of it from some Dutch friends who had lived in Java. Hesse tried agar in his nutrient tubes and found that it worked much better than gelatin. He wrote to Robert Koch about his discovery, and Koch rapidly adapted agar to his own studies. In his short paper on tuberculosis published in 1882, Koch mentioned using agar as a solidifying agent. No formal paper on the use of agar was ever published.

The Petri Plate

One final extension of the plate technique should be mentioned here: the development by Richard J. Petri (1852–1921) of a special plate for agar or gelatin culture. In Koch's original method, flat glass plates were used which were layered with nutrient gelatin or agar on a special horizontal pouring apparatus. The poured plates were then placed on small glass shelves under a large bell jar for incubation. The glass plates and the bell jar were cumbersome, and the pouring apparatus involving a complex arrangement.

Petri's enhancement, which turned out to be amazingly useful, was the development of the special glass plate which bears his name. The plates that Petri first used were flat double-sided dishes of 10–11 cm in diameter and 1–1.5 cm in height. The dishes were sterilized separately from the medium by dry heat, and after cooling, the nutrient agar was poured in. The medium solidified in a few hours and the plates could then be used. Petri noted that such plates dried out slowly, could be easily examined directly under the microscope, and colonies could be readily seen through the bottom of the dish. He especially noted the value of these plates for carrying out quantitative counts of bacteria.

Significance of the Plate Technique

The far-reaching implications of the Koch plate technique are obvious to all bacteriologists. Perhaps no technique has had such an important influence on the development of the field. When we contemplate this miracle now, we might wonder why the plate technique had not been thought of earlier. Certainly one of the major reasons was that earlier workers lacked the will to develop new techniques. As long as one had doubts about the germ theory of disease, there was little motivation for thinking up new techniques. But Koch was strongly committed, and he realized the importance of the pure culture. . . . And it was so simple to me that anyone could learn it. Even the French, who found themselves at odds with much of Koch's work, acknowledged the significance of Koch's plate technique. As Pasteur's closest associate Émile Roux said:

> Culture in solid media is very useful because it permits us to observe the form of the colonies and because it readily permits the separation of diverse organisms.

Soon workers from all over the world were flocking to Koch's door to learn his techniques. . . . [Koch also went] to London, where he introduced the plate technique to Lister and Pasteur, certainly a memorable occasion in the history of bacteriology.

Identifying the Virus

By Milton Zaitlin

Milton Zaitlin is professor emeritus in plant pathology at Cornell University. His work has focused on the generation of virus-resistant plants, and he has tried to educate the public about the risks and benefits of plant genetic engineering. In the following article, Zaitlin discusses the first record of a virus—an infectious agent so small that it escaped detection by nineteenth-century microscopes. As Zaitlin explains, at the end of the nineteenth century, many bacteriologists were convinced that diseases could be assigned to microbes. But in 1879, one reported infectious tobacco plant disease seemed to have no microbial contagion. Adolf Mayer, a Dutch scientist, studied the transmission of the disease, but could not trace its origin. In the next decade, a Russian scientist, Dmitrii Iwanowski, followed Mayer's experiments in hopes of explaining the cause of the tobacco disease. He found that the contagion resisted attempts to isolate it by filtration, even with the ultrafine porcelain filters that trapped all known bacteria. He did not, however, conclude that the contagion was so small—smaller than common bacteria—that it could evade filtration. As Zaitlin maintains, that conclusion was reached by Martinus Beijerinck, a Dutchman, in 1898 after repeating the filtration experiments. Beijerinck insisted that the agent, which he termed a *filterable virus* (Latin for poison), was smaller than a bacteria, thus making the important discovery that not all contagions were filterable bacteria.

To appreciate the discovery of the new infectious agent, the virus, at the end of the 19th century, we must think within the context of what was known about disease etiology at that time. It had only been appreciated for a short time that many diseases were caused by infectious entities. The work of pioneers like [Louis] Pasteur, [Joseph] Lister and [Robert] Koch had brought an appreciation of the causal agents of anthrax and tuberculosis. The dogma of the day was firmly entrenched in the postulates of Koch, who described in detail what was essential in order to establish the causal organism for a disease: 1) The organism must be associated with the pathological relationship to the disease and its symptoms; 2) The organism must be isolated and obtained in pure culture; 3) Inoculation of the organism from the pure culture must reproduce the disease; and 4) The organism must be recovered once again from the lesions of the host. A further and dominant consideration in the thinking of microbiologists was the belief that most infectious organisms would not pass through a filter of unglazed porcelain. Microbiologists and pathologists were confident that a microorganism would be identifiable for each infectious disease, and that it could be seen under the microscope.

The discovery saga of tobacco mosaic virus (TMV) begins with Adolf Mayer, Director of the Agricultural Experiment Station at Wageningen in The Netherlands. Mayer's attention was first called to study the peculiar disease of tobacco in 1879. Although known since the middle of the 19th century in the literature, he is considered to be the first person to transmit tobacco mosaic by using the juice extracted from a diseased plant as the inoculum to infect other plants. His paper, published in 1886, in addition to describing the disease and its symptoms in detail, lists his attempts to ascertain the causal agent of the malady.

The disease which he named tobacco mosaic, was a serious impediment to tobacco growing, and he wrote that in some places it has ". . . caused the cultivation of tobacco to be given up entirely. . . ." He noted the symptoms of the disease, but as he observed healthy plants interspersed among diseased ones, he stated that "It may be accepted for certain, that an obviously diseased plant is never a source of infection for its surroundings." This observation contradicts current experience, and is also at variance with his own transmission studies.

Early Studies of TMV

Mayer's studies encompassed a comparative chemical analysis of healthy and diseased leaves to see if a difference in nutrition could explain the disease. Similarly, analyses of soil in which diseased plants were grown and the presence of nematodes in those soils failed to reveal the cause. He investigated temperature, light, fertilization, looked for fungi or "animal parasites." "Then I suddenly made the discovery that the juice from diseased plants obtained by grinding was a certain infectious substance for healthy plants." This exciting discovery prompted a careful look at the inoculum source for "protoplasmic bodies . . . taken up with special zeal." He tried to follow Koch's postulates, and indeed, was able to culture organisms from the extracts, but of course, none of these would reproduce the disease. He tried to reproduce the disease by inoculation with a number of well-known bacteria and fluids, such as manures from several animals, including man, grated old cheese and putrefied legumes. He was left with the conclusion that the infectious agent was either an enzyme, or some sort of microorganism. He thought it absurd to think it was an enzyme, as it would not be able to reproduce itself. He did experiments with filter paper, and found the agent passed through initially, but upon repeated filtration, in which a "clear filtrate" is obtained, the extract was not infectious, and concluded that the infectious agent was a bacterium. (He ruled out fungi, as he considered that they would not pass through even the first filtration with paper.) This is a strange result, as with current experience with TMV, one would not expect that it would be retained by filter paper; it takes nitrocellulose or similar filters of very small pore size to retain it. Although Mayer came to the wrong conclusion about his finding, he died in 1942 at age 99 which would have given him adequate opportunity to see the modern concept of the virus develop, including its purification of the virus by [Wendel Meredith] Stanley in 1935.

The Infectious Agent of TMV

The man most often given credit for the discovery of the nature of the infectious agent . . . was Dmitrii Iwanowski (sometimes transliterated as Ivanowski or Ivanovsky). However, Martinus Beijerinck should be given credit [since,] in contrast to Iwanowski, he appreciated the significance of his findings.

Iwanowski presented his findings to the Academy of Science in St. Petersburg (Russia) in 1892. He disputed the findings of Mayer with respect to the filterability of the agent of tobacco mosaic disease through double filter paper. He did a number of filtration experiments of his own, using porcelain Chamberland filter-candles, which were considered to be the ultimate test for bacteria, as they would be retained on the filter. He was surprised by the result and suspected a defective filter could explain the agent's filterability, but convinced himself by further testing of the filters that they were not defective.

"According to the opinions prevalent today, it seems to me that the latter is to be explained most simply by the assumption of a toxin secreted by the bacteria present, which is dissolved in the filtered sap. Besides this there is another equally acceptable explanation possible, namely, that the bacteria of the tobacco plant penetrated through the pores of the Chamberland filter-candles, even though before every experiment I checked the filter used in the usual manner and convinced myself of the absence of fine leaks and openings."

Iwanowski had one final publication on TMV in 1903. In contrast to his earlier very short paper, this one was a detailed description of the disease, including microscopic observations on the two types of inclusions found in cells of infected tissues, and made extensive unsuccessful efforts to culture the agent. Nevertheless, he still came to the conclusion that the causal agent was an unculturable bacterium. He was aware, however, of the report of Beijerinck, but that did not sway him from the above conclusion.

The Infectious Agent Is a Filterable Virus

The article by Martinus Beijerinck, published in 1898 is very insightful and is the most detailed on the disease and its causal agent. Of the three reports considered here, it is by far the most detailed and innovative in its approach to the study of the tobacco mosaic disease.

Beijerinck looked for "microbes" associated with the disease, and could find none. He repeated the filtration experiments of his predecessors (although he was apparently unaware of the work of Iwanowski) and concluded that what passed through porcelain filters remained infectious and was sterile of microorganisms. He concluded that it was a "contagium vivum fluidum," a contagious living fluid. He found that from the sap of a diseased plant, ". . . an infinite number of healthy plants may be inoculated and infected . . ." and concluded that the infectious agent reproduces itself in the diseased plants. To demonstrate that the infectious agent was not a microbe, he conducted diffusion experiments, in which he allowed the "virus" to penetrate an agar plate. He found that indeed it could penetrate ". . . to no small depth." He found that the agent diffused about 2 mm in 10 days, and concluded that the virus was soluble, which indeed it is. He found that the infectious extract was stable during a three month test, but the virulence did not increase or decrease in the extract, further evidence that it was not bacterial. He also observed that the virus remains viable, without loss ". . . in strength of infection . . ." even after the tissue is dried, but that heating the extract to 90° inactivated it.

Beijerinck studied the disease itself in detail using his capacity to transmit it as a means of deciding the presence or absence of virus. He concluded, based on symptomatology [observable evidence of disease], that only young leaves could be infected, and concluded that only coils which are dividing can become infected—certainly not the case, as it is now known that old leaves may become infected, but rarely show symptoms. He correctly deduced that the virus moved within the plant. . . .

[Dutch molecular biologist Johannes] Bos contends that credit for the discovery of TMV as a virus should go to Beijerinck. He argues that even in his exhaustive 1903 paper, based on his thesis, Iwanowski did not appreciate the significance of his finding. He still argued in favor of a bacterial etiology, and felt that spores of the causal organism were able to pass through the filter. Beijerinck, on the other hand, did appreciate that he has something quite different from microbes and Bos feels that for that reason, he deserves credit for developing the viral concept.

Nevertheless, whomever is the one history will record as the discoverer of the virus concept, these three gentlemen are to be remembered for their insights into the investigations to find the causal agent for a puzzling disease. Tobacco mosaic virus has been very important in the history of virology for many reasons beyond the discovery of the viral concept. It was the first to be purified and many fundamental concepts of virology were developed with it. The chemical composition of the virus, the isolation of its protein and nucleic acid components, its immunogenicity [ability to produce an immune system response], infectious RNA [ribonucleic acid], reconstitution from its dissociated parts, the first determination of the sequence of a viral coat protein are among the milestones.

CHAPTER 2

The War Against Germs

Proving That a Bacterium Can Cause Human Disease

By Thomas D. Brock

World-class microbiologist Thomas D. Brock published several books, including *Milestones in Microbiology*, a biography of scientist Robert Koch, and a history of bacterial genetics. He is also the architect of the first seven editions of *Biology of Microorganisms*, which is now called *Brock's Biology of Microorganisms*. In the following excerpt from his biography of Koch, Brock outlines in detail the first proof that a bacterium causes disease in humans. Koch's discovery that a rod-shaped bacterium (a bacillus) caused tuberculosis revolutionized the study of infectious disease by proving that contagious human disease could be caused by bacteria. It also improved the ability to manage and treat tuberculosis patients and brought the study of bacteriology into the realm of medicine and public health. The method of Koch's discovery outlined for the scientific community the research protocol necessary for establishing disease causation. This protocol has since been termed "Koch's postulates," and is still used today. According to these postulates, an organism must first be isolated from the diseased individual. Then, the organism must be isolated and grown in pure culture. Then, a pure culture of that organism must be inoculated into a healthy individual. That inoculated individual must develop the same disease, and then the same types of organisms must be isolated from the newly diseased individual. If this process can be demonstrated and reproduced, then the organism is proved to be the cause of the disease.

Thomas D. Brock, *Robert Koch: A Life in Medicine and Bacteriology*. Washington, DC: ASM Press, 1999. Copyright © 1999 by the American Society for Microbiology. All rights reserved. Reproduced by permission.

t is fair to say that no single discovery in infectious disease has had more wide-reaching influence than Koch's discovery of the causal agent of tuberculosis. At the time Koch began his work, one-seventh of all reported deaths of human beings were ascribed to tuberculosis, and if one considered only the productive middle-age groups, one-third of the deaths were due to this dread disease. And the disease was not limited to any socioeconomic group, attacking equally rich and poor. In [English religious writer] John Bunyan's famous phrase, tuberculosis was the "Captain of the Men of Death."

The impressive thing about Koch's work on tuberculosis was not only its scientific brilliance, but the *speed* with which it was accomplished. He began the first experiments on 18 August 1881. And on 24 March 1882, less than 8 months later, he gave his famous and historic lecture on the tubercle bacillus to the Berlin Physiological Society, a lecture which was published only three weeks later.

The Background on Tuberculosis

Tuberculosis had been recognized as a specific disease entity since antiquity. There is evidence of tuberculosis lesions in the bones of Egyptian mummies. Although tuberculosis of the lungs does not seem to have been common in Egypt, *pulmonary tuberculosis* (also called *phthisis*) was well recognized by the Greeks, and extensive descriptions can be found in the writings of Hippocrates and others. Another major form of tuberculosis was subsequently recognized, *miliary tuberculosis*, in which the lesions are tiny nodules disseminated throughout the body. By the early 19th century, pathology was a well-developed discipline, but many pathologists held the view that miliary tuberculosis and phthisis were two distinct diseases. . . . The French pathologist René Laennec held, on the other hand, that miliary tuberculosis and phthisis were two aspects of the same disease, and that tuberculosis was a morbid process that could occur in various parts of the body. According to Laennec, phthisis (called consumption in England) was tuberculosis of the lungs.

At the time Koch initiated his work, there was strong evidence that tuberculosis was a contagious disease. The French physician Jean Antoine Villemin (1827–1892) had shown in 1865 that tuberculosis was transmissible to experimental animals, a discovery that was amply confirmed by [other scientists]. But the suspected causal organism had never been seen, either in diseased tissues or in culture.

Seeing the Tubercle Bacillus

When Koch began his work, he knew from Villemin of the value of the experimental animal for tuberculosis studies and he had access to extensive pathological material from the "phthisis ward" at the Berlin Charité Hospital. Koch's aim, from the beginning, was the demonstration of a parasite as the causal agent of tuberculosis. To this end, he employed all of the methods that he had so carefully developed over the previous six years: microscopy, staining of tissues, pure culture isolation, animal inoculation. These methods, which worked so well with anthrax and wound infections, also worked with tuberculosis, but not without great difficulty. The causal agent of tuberculosis was exceedingly difficult to stain and visualize in diseased tissues, and it grew so slowly in culture.

As is now well known, *Mycobacterium tuberculosis*, the tubercle bacillus, is very difficult to stain with conventional bacteriological stains because of its extremely waxy nature. One of Koch's main contributions was the discovery of a method for staining the tubercle bacillus. . . . [He used methylene blue to stain a sample. Then he used a second, brown dye before photographing the sample. The two dyes gave the images a unique contrast that made them easy to analyze.] The staining of the tubercle bacillus . . . was the key which opened the door to the mystery of this disease. Once the organism could be readily demonstrated in infected tissues, microscopy could be used to follow experimental inoculations and as an aid in cultivation. And subsequently, the staining procedure proved invaluable as a diagnostic and public health method.

Koch recognized quickly that the peculiar staining properties of the tubercle bacillus indicated something unusual about the cellular properties of the organism. Even in his first work he stated:

It seems likely that the tubercle bacillus is surrounded with a special wall of unusual properties, and that the penetration of a dye through this wall can only occur when alkali, aniline, or a similar substance is present.

The bacteria visualized by my technique show many distinct characteristics. They are rod-shaped and belong therefore to the group of bacilli. They are very thin and are only one-fourth to one-half as long as the diameter of a red blood cell, but can occasionally reach a length as long as the diameter of a red cell. They possess a form and size which is surprisingly like that of the leprosy bacillus.

The Tubercle Bacillus Is Constantly Present When Tuberculosis Is Present

Using his newly developed staining method, Koch proceeded to make a careful microscopic survey of tuberculous tissues. As noted, he had access to excellent clinical material at the Charité Hospital, which was near his institute:

> In all tissues in which the tuberculosis process has recently developed and is progressing most rapidly, these bacilli can be found in large numbers. They ordinarily form small groups of cells which are pressed together and arranged in bundles, and frequently are lying within tissue cells. . . . Many times the bacteria occur in large numbers outside of cells as well. Especially at the edge of large, cheesy masses, the bacilli occur almost exclusively in large numbers free of the tissue cells.

> As soon as the peak of the tubercle eruption has passed, the bacilli become rarer, but occur still in small groups or singly at the edge of the tubercle mass, with many lightly stained and almost invisible bacilli, which are probably in the process of dying or are already dead. . . .

> Because of the quite regular occurrence of the tubercle bacilli, it must seem surprising that they have never been seen before. This can be explained, however, by the fact that the bacilli are extremely small structures, and are generally in such small numbers that they would elude the most attentive observer without the use of a special staining reaction. . . .

> On the basis of my extensive observations, I consider it as proved that in all tuberculous conditions of man and animals there exists a characteristic bacterium which I have designated as the tubercle bacillus, which has specific properties which allow it to be distinguished from all other microorganisms.

The Culture of the Tubercle Bacillus

Koch was well aware that the *presence* of the organism did not, of itself indicate that it was the *cause* of the disease entity:

> In order to prove that tuberculosis is brought about by the tubercle bacillus, and is a definite parasitic disease brought about by the growth and reproduction of these same bacilli, the bacilli must be isolated from the body, and cultured so long in pure culture that they are freed from any diseased production of the animal organism which may still be adhering to the bacilli. After this, the isolated bacilli must bring about the transfer of the disease to other animals, and cause the same disease picture which can be brought about through the inoculation of healthy animals with naturally developing tubercular materials.

This statement, the clearest Koch had yet written of what was to be later considered part of his "postulates," sets out the research protocol that would be needed. . . .

Koch had spent the past six years developing his culture methods for bacterial pathogens, and by this time he had perfected his plate technique. It must have seemed that it would be a straightforward problem to remove tuberculous tissue from either patients or experimental animals, place the tissue on culture media, and incubate. However, what worked well for anthrax and wound infections did not work for the tubercle bacillus. The organism grew at best very slowly. It did not grow at all at room temperature, while at body temperature the nutrient gelatin that was commonly used liquefied. Also, although the nutritional requirements are not complex, the organism is very sensitive to the presence of inhibitory agents, and therefore behaves as a rather fastidious organism. After many trials, Koch hit on a method using coagulated blood serum. The blood serum served as the source of nutrients, and by coagulating the serum in tubes, it was possible to produce a solid medium upon which colonies could be obtained. By allowing the serum to harden while the test tubes were in a slanted position, a large surface area for culture was obtained.

Using this procedure, Koch removed tuberculous tissues from experimental animals and aseptically inoculated serum slants. We can marvel at the persistence he showed in this study. On coagulated blood serum incubated at 37–38°C, no growth of tubercle bacilli was seen at all during the first week, but after the second week, tiny colonies, very small, dry, and scale-like, appeared. If any growth was obtained in the first several days, it was almost certainly due to contaminants and the experiment was considered a failure. Only colonies appearing slowly, at some time during the second week, were likely to represent tubercle bacilli. However, these colonies could generally already be seen at the end of the first week if a 30–40 power microscope was used. After 10–14 days, the culture was transferred to fresh medium using a sterilized platinum wire. . . .

The Pure Cultures Are Virulent

Now came the most critical part of Koch's study—the proof that the pure cultures obtained from tuberculous material caused the disease. Here, Koch was greatly benefitted by the fact that guinea pigs can be readily infected with the tubercle bacillus, even though these animals never succumb to tuberculosis naturally:

A substance can be tested for its virulence by inoculating four to six guinea pigs with it, after making use of all precautions, such as previously disinfecting the site of inoculation, using sterile instruments, etc. The results are uniformly the same. In all animals which are inoculated with fresh masses containing tubercle bacilli . . . the animals become progressively weaker and die after four to six weeks. . . . In the organs of all of these animals . . . the recognizable changes due to tuberculosis occur. That these changes in guinea pigs are due solely to the inoculation of material containing the tubercle bacilli can be seen from experiments in which inoculation was performed with scrofulous glands or fungus masses from joints, in which no tubercle bacilli could be found. In these cases, not a single animal became sick, while animals inoculated with bacilli-containing material always showed an extensive infection with tuberculosis after four weeks.

Up until now my studies have shown that a characteristic bacillus is always associated with tuberculosis, and that these bacilli can be obtained from tuberculous organs and isolated in pure culture. It now remained to prove the most important question, namely, that the isolated bacilli are able to bring about the typical tuberculosis disease process when inoculated again into animals. . . .

When Koch inoculated animals with his pure cultures, they succumbed to tuberculosis, with the same symptoms and pathology seen in animals inoculated with material from human cases.

The results of a number of experiments with bacillus cultures inoculated into a large number of animals, and inoculated in different ways, all have led to the same results. . . .

All of these facts taken together lead to the conclusion that the bacilli which are present in the tuberculous substances not only accompany the tuberculosis process, but are the cause of it. In the bacillus we have, therefore, the actual tubercle virus.

We must consider the work on the tubercle bacillus to be Koch's masterpiece and the culmination of all the work he had done before. . . .

The Announcement of Discovery

Robert Koch first announced his discovery of the tubercle bacillus at a lecture he gave to the Berlin Physiological Society on the evening of 24 March 1882. . . .

Before his lecture, Koch set out on the table his microscopic preparations, more than 200 of them. He had brought everything with him, his microscope, test tubes with cultures, Erlenmeyer flasks, small square glass boxes containing cultures, pathological material preserved in alcohol. The table was eventually filled with small white plates, each containing a culture. The room was full to overflowing. The lecture proceeded slowly and carefully, Koch laying out for his audience his strongly convincing evidence of the tubercle bacillus.

When Koch finished his lecture, there was silence. No applause, no questions, no debate. Those who attended the lecture remembered later the silence, not of boredom or doubt, but of stunned admiration at the brilliant work they had just heard. Slowly, a few members of the audience rose and shook hands with Koch. Then others began to examine his preparations, his pure cultures, and his other demonstrations. [German medical professor] Paul Ehrlich, one of the most important attendees, and an expert on staining bacteria, sank to the stool by the microscope and fell deep into contemplation as he examined the preparations. Later, he was to remark:

I hold that evening to be the most important experience of my scientific life.

Three weeks later Koch's short paper was published in the Berliner Klinische Wochenschrift. It created a sensation throughout the world. . . .

The Acceptance of Koch's Work on Tuberculosis

Koch had predicted that it would take a year of hard fighting to convince the medical world of the validity of his work. He was wrong. Despite a few exceptions, his work was rapidly accepted. The results of Koch's lecture spread quickly through medical circles of Berlin. Numerous physicians streamed to the Physiological Institute over the next few days after the lecture to observe the microscopic preparations that were left in place. Even the eminent German pathologist Rudolf Virchow appeared, and although remaining dubious (in his subsequent lectures on tuberculosis he used the phrase "so-called tubercle bacillus") he did admit that Koch had something.

As we have noted, tuberculosis manifests itself in the body in a variety of ways. Pathologists such as Virchow had carefully described, on morphological grounds, these various conditions. Now, examining Koch's microscopic preparations, Virchow and others could readily convince themselves that in *all* of these conditions, the same bacterium was present. The discovery of the tubercle bacillus made possible a unified theory of tuberculosis, in all its manifestations. And because the organism was so characteristic, it was hard to doubt the validity of Koch's conclusions. . . .

The impact of Koch's work on both public health and bacteriology was enormous. By showing that the "Captain of the Men of Death" was a bacterial disease, Koch had made bacteriology one of the most important disciplines of medicine. And by providing a diagnostic procedure of exquisite sensitivity, Koch placed the management of tuberculosis patients on a scientific footing.

Proving That a Virus Can Cause Human Disease

By the Walter Reed Army Medical Center

The Walter Reed Army Medical Center published the following brief biography of U.S. Army surgeon Walter Reed. Reed began studying medicine in 1868. He obtained two medical degrees, did internships in New York hospitals, and served on the boards of health in New York and Brooklyn. Looking for financial security, Reed decided to join the U.S. Army in 1874. After fifteen years of service as a family doctor for army personnel, Reed was sent to Baltimore where he had the opportunity to study bacteriology and pathology under Dr. William Henry Welch, a former student of the famous French scientist Louis Pasteur. Since these subjects were not taught as part of the medical curriculum of that day, Reed was one of the few U.S. researchers with the necessary background for studying the cause of infectious diseases. In May 1900, Reed was appointed to lead the army's Yellow Fever Commission, charged with the task of studying and controlling yellow fever during the American invasion of Cuba in the Spanish-American War. In less than two years, Reed and fellow board members were able to prove that the mosquito was the intermediate host for the yellow fever agent and that the agent—the cause of the disease—was a filterable virus. This was the first confirmation that a virus could cause disease in humans.

I n May 1900 Major Walter Reed was appointed president of a board whose purpose it was to study infectious diseases in Cuba paying particular attention to yellow fever. The other members of the board were Acting Assistant Surgeons Major

Walter Reed Army Medical Center, "Major Walter Reed, Medical Corps, U.S. Army," www.wramc.amedd.army.mil, 2004.

James Carroll, Major Jesse W. Lazear and Major Aristides Agramonte of Havana. As a result of this Yellow Fever Board, very few people living today have any knowledge of this dread disease.

Yellow fever killed more men in the Spanish-American War than did the enemy. It appeared in Central America in 1596, probably imported from Africa by slave ships. It may have been the disease from which members of Columbus' second expedition suffered in 1495. Ninety epidemics struck the United States between 1596 and 1900. In 1793 an epidemic first hit Philadelphia, then the U.S. capital, causing the Government to flee as ten per cent of the population perished. [George] Washington went to Mount Vernon while [Thomas] Jefferson fled the disorder caused by the onslaught of the disease. Because of frequent epidemics which destroyed ninety per cent of his expeditionary forces in 1802, [French emperor] Napoleon was influenced to sell the Louisiana Territory [to the United States]. It was chiefly because of "yellow jack," as the disease was nicknamed from the penant which was flown during quarantine, that the French were unable to complete the Panama Canal. The danger of contaminating the southern states was considered to be a major factor in the annexation of Cuba.

The onset of yellow fever came with chills and a headache. Then followed severe pains in the back, arms and legs accompanied by high fever and vomiting. The feverish stage might last hours, days, or weeks. Jaundice, from which the fever derives its name, might then appear. Then came the so-called "stage of calm" when the severity of the symptoms subsided and the fever dropped. In less serious cases this stage indicated recovery. But in the main, this stage was followed by a return of the fever accompanied by internal bleeding which caused the dreaded "black vomit" when blood released into the stomach was ejected.

Reed and Carroll had estimated that there were 300,000 cases in the United States between 1793 and 1900, which cost the nation almost $500,000,000 with a mortality rate usually at forty per cent but sometimes as high as eighty-five per cent. The scourge of yellow fever had plagued the southeastern United States for two hundred years, but nowhere was it more prevalent than in Havana. Surgeon General George Miller Sternberg was this country's leading expert on yellow fever. Because neither he nor other researchers had been able to pinpoint the specific cause, he was astounded to hear the claim of Dr. Giuseppe Sanarelli, who in 1897 stated quite conclusively that the fever was caused by Bacillus icteroides.

Studies in Cuba

On June 25, 1901, Walter Reed arrived at Columbia Barracks in Quemados about six miles from Havana. Major Reed attended Major Jefferson R. Kean, Chief Surgeon of the Department of Western Cuba, who had himself contracted the disease and fortunately recovered. Then Doctor James Carroll and Major Reed set out enthusiastically to prove Sanarelli's theory. By August 1900, however, they had found no causal relationship between Bacillus icteroides, a member of the hog-cholera group, and yellow fever.

The Board then turned its attention to the theory of Dr. Carlos Juan Finlay and examined it more carefully. For nineteen years this resident of Havana had contended that yellow fever was carried in the body of a common house mosquito which at that time was called Culex fasciatus, later Stegomyia fasciata, and is now known as Aedes aegypti. This theory had been expounded even earlier, but it was Finlay who was its staunchest exponent. However, after some 100 experimental inoculations had failed to produce any cases of the disease under strict laboratory control, Finlay was scoffed at; people referred to him as the "mosquito man." There was evidence, however, that tended to lend credence to this theory which even the Yellow Fever Board, optimistic though it was, had doubted. First of all, the disease skipped erratically from house to house, jumping around corners. One member of a household might contract the disease while others in close contact never became ill or did so after a period of about two weeks had elapsed. This was quite unlike any other infectious disease except malaria which had already been shown to be spread by the Anopheles mosquito.

Studying the Means of Disease Transmission

The Board then decided that the best way to study yellow fever was not by searching for a specific agent but rather by identifying the means by which the fever was transmitted. For this purpose Major Reed organized the Board in the following manner: Major Reed himself was in charge of the entire project; Dr. James Carroll was in charge of bacteriology; Dr. Jesse W. Lazear was in charge of the experimental mosquitoes; and Dr. Aristedes Agramonte was in charge of pathology.

Dr. Lazear had recently been working with malaria mosquitoes and attacked his duties with great enthusiasm in view of the information he read concerning the observations of Dr. Henry R. Carter of the Marine Hospital Service (now the Public Health Service). Dr. Carter had observed that it took two or three weeks for the first case of yellow fever to produce the next case in a community. On the basis of this observation, he suspected that an insect might be the intermediary since this would account for the delay in transmission as the disease ripened in the mosquito. Dr. Finlay had given some of the black, cigar-shaped eggs to the Board, and Lazear allowed them to hatch. It wasn't difficult to maintain a supply since the mosquitoes bred in any clean, still water. Dr. Carroll then volunteered to be bitten and promptly developed a successful case of yellow fever which was experimentally defective since there may have been other sources of contamination. Carroll luckily recovered and went on with his work in bacteriology. Next, Lazear asked Private William Dean of Ohio if he would consent to be bitten. Answering that he wasn't "afraid of any little old gnat" Dean permitted the female Aedes aegypti to dine on him. He developed the first successful case and recovered. Dr. Lazear allowed himself to be bitten and, after several days of delirium and black vomit, died—a true martyr to science. He had been working in Las Animas Hospital in Havana.

Major Reed, although grieved at Lazear's death, was excited at the prospect of successfully tracking down the secret of the fever. Dr. Lazear's notebook, found by Lieutenant Albert E. Truby (later Brigadier General), yielded the key. In it, through the carefully recorded controlled experiments, Walter Reed found that in order for a mosquito to become infected, it had to bite a yellow fever patient during the first three days of his illness; only during that time was the agent present in the bloodstream. Further, it required at least twelve days for the agent to ripen in the female mosquito (only the female aegypti draws blood) and migrate to her salivary glands before the fever could be passed to another person.

In October 1900, Major Reed was able to announce to the annual meeting of the American Public Health Association that "the mosquito serves as the intermediate host for the parasite of yellow fever."

Experiments on Human Volunteers

These two cases, although sufficient to convince the Yellow Fever Board that they were at last experiencing some success, were not enough for the thorough scientific mind of Walter Reed, nor would they be for a public which the press had instructed in the "foolishness" of the mosquito theory. With the express permission of General Leonard Wood, Governor General of Cuba, Camp Lazear, named for their fallen comrade, was established on November 20, 1900. Moreover, General Wood authorized the Board to use and pay American and Spanish volunteers for the experiments since at this time yellow fever was thought to be a disease afflicting only humans. Dr. Carroll had exhausted the list of experimental animals, rats and the like normally used for scientific research, failing to produce any cases of the fever in them. In addition to the mosquito theory, Dr. Reed also desired to disprove the seemingly fallacious belief that yellow fever could be transmitted and induced from clothing and bedding soiled by the excrement of yellow fever sufferers. These articles were known as fomites and were commonly thought to carry the disease. Just as "everybody knew" that the mosquito theory was foolish, so "everybody knew" that fomites were dangerous.

In November 1900, Camp Lazear was established one mile from Quemados and placed under strict quarantine. At his experimental station Private John R. Kissinger permitted himself to be bitten and promptly developed the first case of controlled experimental yellow fever. This case has been deemed as important to medical science as Robert Koch's discovery of the tubercle bacillus and the development of the diphtheria anti-toxin. Kissinger and John J. Moran had volunteered on condition that they would receive no gratuities, performing their service "solely in the interest of science and the cause of humanity."

Then, in order to prove the theory for all time and to destroy the fomite myth, two specially constructed buildings were erected in Camp Lazear. Building Number One, or the "Infected Clothing Building," was composed of one room, 14×20 feet heated by a stove to ninety-five degrees. For twenty nights Dr. Robert P. Cooke and Privates Folk and Jernegan hung offensive clothing and beefing around the walls. They slept on sheets and pillows befouled by the blood and vomit of yellow fever victims. Not one of the volunteers contracted the disease. On December 19, 1900, they were relieved by Privates Hanberry and England who, in turn, were finally relieved by Privates Hildebrand and Andrus. From November 30, 1900, to January 10, 1901, the experiment ran to completion, disproving the fomite theory of transmission and thereby demonstrating the uselessness of destroying the personal effects of yellow fever victims, thus saving thousands of dollars in property.

The second building was similarly constructed and was called the "Infected Mosquito Building." It was divided into two parts separated by a screen with screens on the windows as well. Mr. John Moran, a clerk in General Fitzhugh Lee's office, was bitten by fifteen infected mosquitoes, developed the fever and recovered. The other volunteers who were separated, and thereby protected by the screen, escaped infection. Ten cases were produced in this manner.

The Contagion Is in the Blood

Yellow fever was produced in the bodies of twelve more American and Spanish volunteers either by direct mosquito bites or by injections of infected blood or blood serum. These injections proved that the specific agent of yellow fever is in the blood and that passage through the body of a mosquito is not necessary to its development.

The courage of the volunteers is inestimable. A unique honor helps keep alive the memory of the twenty-four gallant men who participated in this experiment. In 1929 Congress awarded a special gold medal to each man or his next of kin. Had it not been for Major Reed's fair and thoroughly scientific approach to the problem and misconceptions concerning the disease, especially the whole contagion theory, yellow fever might have continued for years. As a result of the Yellow Fever Board's success, Colonel William Crawford Gorgas, then Chief Sanitary Officer for the Department of Cuba, rid the island of this longtime pestilence. Realizing that the mosquitoes never stray far from human dwelling places in order to get their meals of blood necessary for them to lay their eggs, Colonel Gorgas organized inspection parties to check all homes in Havana for possible breeding places, insuring that the only standing water in the homes was needed for family use and properly screened. All other water receptacles were to be emptied. Later he applied the same techniques in the [Panama] Canal Zone, freeing it of fever, permitting the United States to complete the Panama Canal so vital for commerce and deployment of the Pacific fleet. Thus the menace which had struck the United States every year since 1648, from Pensacola to Nantucket Island, was eradicated. There would be no more epidemics such as that in Memphis in 1878 which cost the country one hundred million dollars.

In February 1901, Walter Reed returned to the United States where he was an instant success in medical circles. All through the acclaim he remained modest and reserved. His constant hope of doing something to relieve the suffering of mankind had been fulfilled; his dedication to duty, sound judgment, and thorough scientific methods was an inspiration to the deans of medical research.

The Contagion Is a Filterable Virus

In the summer of 1901, Dr. Carroll proved that the specific agent of yellow fever was sub-microscopic and too small to be caught in the pores of the diatomaceous filter that retained bacteria. Thus the last key to the disease was found. Carroll had proved through a series of inoculations that a filterable virus could cause disease in man. The Board's discoveries were confirmed by the Board of Health of Havana and later a commission of the Pasteur Institute confirmed the agent's filterability. In 1927 it was found that certain species of monkeys were susceptible to the virus, thereby eliminating the need for human subjects. In 1937 a vaccine against yellow fever, called 17-D, was produced by scientists of the International Health Division of the Rockefeller Foundation. The use of this vaccine became routine in the United States Army in 1942. Since yellow fever is still endemic in the jungles of Central America and Africa where anti-mosquito measures are almost impossible, the fever still exists. A distinction is therefore made between "urban" yellow fever which is under control and the jungle variety which persists. As yet there is no cure for the disease, only inoculation against it.

The Golden Age of Microbiology

By Joshua Lederberg

Dr. Joshua Lederberg is an American geneticist and microbiologist who received the Nobel Prize in 1958 for his work in bacterial genetics. His pioneering work has led some to call him the father of molecular genetics. He received the National Medal of Science from President George H.W. Bush in 1989 and has been professor emeritus and Raymond and Beverly Sackler Foundation Scholar at Rockefeller University since 1990. He continues to conduct laboratory research on bacterial and human genetics, and to advise government and industry on global health policy, biological warfare, and the threat of bioterrorism.

In the first half of his article "Infectious History," which is excerpted below, Lederberg presents the development and blossoming of the field of microbiology. Once the germ theory was established in the late nineteenth century, the battle against infectious diseases involved increased attention to bacteriology, virology, vaccination, and antibiotics. As the twentieth century dawned, these fields were institutionalized and microbiology became a much-touted science, with legions of researchers and the support of medical schools and national governments. In the United States, public health organizations carried the work of microbiologists to the population, and many diseases were quickly brought under control. America and other industrialized countries that adopted similar public health measures began to think that infectious diseases would soon be conquered during this golden age of microbiology.

I n 1530, to express his ideas on the origin of syphilis, the Italian physician Girolamo Fracastoro penned *Syphilis, sive morbus Gallicus* (Syphilis, or the French disease) in verse. In it he taught that this sexually transmitted disease was spread by "seeds" distributed by intimate contact. In later writings, he expanded this early "contagionist" theory. Besides contagion by personal contact, he described contagion by indirect contact, such as the handling or wearing of clothes, and even contagion at a distance, that is, the spread of disease by something in the air.

Fracastoro was anticipating, by nearly 350 years, one of the most important turning points in biological and medical history—the consolidation of the germ theory of disease by Louis Pasteur and Robert Koch in the late 1870s. . . . Many people laid the groundwork for the germ theory. Even the terrified masses touched by the Black Death (bubonic plague) in Europe after 1346 had some intimation of a contagion at work. But they lived within a cognitive framework in which scapegoating, say, of witches and Jews, could more "naturally" account for their woes. Breaking that mindset would take many innovations, including microscopy in the hands of Anton van Leeuwenhoek. In 1683, with one of his new microscopes in hand, he visualized bacteria among the animalcules harvested from his own teeth. That opened the way to visualize some of the dreaded microbial agents eliciting contagious diseases.

There were pre-germ-theory advances in therapy, too. Jesuit missionaries in malaria-ridden Peru had noted the native Indians' use of *Cinchona* bark. In 1627, the Jesuits imported the bark (harboring quinine, its anti-infective ingredient) to Europe for treating malaria. Quinine thereby joined the rarified pharmacopoeia—including opium, digitalis, willow (*Salix*) bark with its analgesic salicylates, and little else—that prior to the modern era afforded patients any benefit beyond placebo.

Beginning in 1796, [English doctor] Edward Jenner took another major therapeutic step—the development of vaccination—after observing that milkmaids exposed to cowpox didn't contract smallpox. He had no theoretical insight into the biological mechanism of resistance to the disease, but vaccination became a lasting prophylactic technique on purely empirical grounds. Jenner's discovery had precursors. "Hair of the dog" is an ancient trope for countering injury and may go back to legends of the emperor Mithridates, who habituated himself to lethal doses of poisons by gradually increasing the dose. We now understand more about a host's immunological response to a cross-reacting virus variant.

Sanitary reforms also helped. Arising out of revulsion over the squalor and stink of urban slums in England and the United States, a hygienic movement tried to scrub up dirt and put an end to sewer stenches. The effort had some health impact in the mid–19th century, but it failed to counter diseases spread by fleas and mosquitoes or by personal contact, and it often even failed to keep sewage and drinking water supplies separated.

The Germ Theory

It was the germ theory—which is credited to Pasteur (a chemist by training) and Koch (ultimately a German professor of public health)—that set a new course for studying and contending with infectious disease. Over the second half of the 19th century, these scientists independently synthesized historical evidence with their own research into the germ theory of disease. Pasteur helped reveal the vastness of the microbial world and its many practical applications. He found microbes to be behind the fermentation of sugar into alcohol and the souring of milk. He developed a heat treatment (pasteurization, that is) that killed microorganisms in milk, which then no longer transmitted tuberculosis or typhoid. And he too developed new vaccines. One was a veterinary vaccine against anthrax. Another was against rabies and was first used in humans in 1885 to treat a young boy who had been bitten by a rabid dog.

One of Koch's most important advances was procedural. He articulated a set of logical and experimental criteria, later restated as "Koch's Postulates," as a standard of proof for researchers' assertions that a particular bacterium caused a particular malady. In 1882, he identified the bacterium that causes tuberculosis; a year later he did the same for cholera. Koch also left a legacy of students (and rivals) who began the systematic search for disease-causing microbes: The golden age of microbiology had begun.

Just as the 19th century was ending, the growing world of microbes mushroomed beyond bacteria. In 1892, the Russian microbiologist Dmitri Ivanowski, and in 1898, the Dutch botanist Martinus Beijerinck, discovered exquisitely tiny infectious agents that could pass through bacteria-stopping filters. Too small to be seen with the conventional microscope, these agents were described as "filtrable [*sic*] viruses."

The Golden Age of Microbiology

With a foundation of germ theory in place even before the 20th century, the study of infectious disease was ready to enter a new phase. Microbe hunting became institutionalized, and armies of researchers systematically applied scientific analyses to understanding disease processes and developing therapies.

During the early acme of microbe hunting, from about 1880 to 1940, however, microbes were all but ignored by mainstream biologists. Medical microbiology had a life of its own, but it was almost totally divorced from general biological studies. Pasteur and Koch were scarcely mentioned by the founders of cell biology and genetics. Instead, bacteriology was taught as a specialty in medicine, outside the schools of basic zoology and botany. Conversely, bacteriologists scarcely heard of the conceptual revolutions in genetic and evolutionary theory. . . .

Despite its slow emergence, bacteriology was already having a large impact. Its success is most obviously evidenced by the graying of the population. That public health has been improving—due to many factors, especially our better understanding of infectious agents—is graphically shown by the vital statistics. These began to be diligently recorded in the United States after 1900 in order to guide research and apply it to improving public health. The U.S. experience stands out in charts depicting life expectancy at birth through the century. The average life-span lengthened dramatically: from 47 years in 1900 to [an] expectation of 77 years [in the year 2000] (74 years for males and 80 for females). Similar trends are seen in most other industrialized countries, but the gains have been smaller in economically and socially depressed countries.

Other statistics reveal that the decline in mortality ascribable to infectious disease accounted for almost all of the improvement in longevity up to 1950, when life expectancy had reached 68. The additional decade of life expectancy for babies born today took the rest of the century to gain. Further improvements now appear to be on an asymptotic trajectory: Each new gain is ever harder to come by, at least pending unpredictable breakthroughs in the biology of aging.

The mortality statistics fluctuated considerably during the first half of the last century. Much of this instability was due to sporadic outbreaks of infections such as typhoid fever, tuberculosis, and scarlet fever, which no longer have much statistical impact. Most outstanding is the spike due to the great influenza pandemic of 1918–19 that killed 25 million people worldwide—comparable to the number of deaths in the Great War. Childhood immunization and other science-based medical interventions have played a significant role in the statistical trends also. So have public health measures, among them protection of food and water supplies, segregation of coughing patients, and personal hygiene. Overall economic growth has also helped by contributing to less crowded housing, improved working conditions (including sick leave), and better nutrition.

As infectious diseases have assumed lower rankings in mortality statistics, other killers—mostly diseases of old age, affluence, and civilization—have moved up the ladder. Heart disease and cancer, for example, have loomed as larger threats over the past few decades. Healthier lifestyles, including less smoking, sparer diets, more exercise, and better hygiene, have been important countermeasures. Prophylactic medications such as aspirin, as well as medical and surgical interventions, have also kept people alive longer.

The 1950s were notable for the "wonder drugs"—the new antibiotics penicillin, streptomycin, chloramphenicol, and a growing list of others that at times promised an end to bacteria-based disease. Viral pathogens have offered fewer routes to remedies, except for vaccines, such as Jonas Salk's and Albert Sabin's polio vaccines. These worked by priming immune systems for later challenges by the infectious agents. Old vaccines, including Jenner's smallpox vaccine, also were mobilized in massive public health campaigns, sometimes with fantastic results. By the end of the 1970s, smallpox became the first disease to be eradicated from the human experience.

Confidence about medicine's ability to fight infectious disease had grown so high by the mid-1960s that some optimists were portraying infectious microbes as largely conquered. They suggested that researchers shift their attention to constitutional scourges of heart disease, cancer, and psychiatric disorders. These views were reflected in the priorities for research funding and pharmaceutical development. President Nixon's 1971 launch of a national crusade against cancer, which tacitly implied that cancer could be conquered by the bicentennial celebrations of 1976, was an example. Few people now sustain the illusion that audacious medical goals like conquering cancer or infectious disease can be achieved by short-term campaigns.

Developing Antibiotics to Fight Disease

By Andrew J. Schuman

Dr. Andrew J. Schuman practices pediatrics in New Hampshire and is adjunct assistant professor of pediatrics at Dartmouth Medical School. He is a contributing editor for the journal *Contemporary Pediatrics* and wrote the following article to summarize the history of antimicrobial therapy and remind physicians not to abuse the power of these healing drugs. As Schuman relates, prior to the discovery and production of antibiotics, many children died of diseases such as typhoid, cholera, croup, scarlet fever, diphtheria, and whooping cough. Many other children suffered horrible treatments to try to cure these diseases. Once it was proven that specific organisms caused specific diseases, the search for "magic bullets" that would destroy the organisms, but not the patient, began. In the early 1900s, the first such bullet was discovered and marketed to treat syphilis. Then in the 1930s, the first sulfa drugs were introduced to fight streptococcal infections. In the next decade, English researchers developed and marketed penicillin. The success of penicillin during World War II fueled the pharmaceutical industry. Penicillin modifications and other antibiotics were developed. In the same way that microbe hunters looked for germs that caused infectious diseases, antibiotic researchers began systematically studying bacteria and fungi to determine which ones produced antimicrobial cures that would be effective for humans. As Schuman notes, the result of these efforts has armed physicians with powerfully healing drugs, and the vigilant use of these drugs will hopefully maintain their effectiveness.

Andrew J. Schuman, "A Concise History of Antimicrobial Therapy (Serendipity and All): Some Brilliant Observations and More than a Little Luck Have Given Physicians Their Most Powerful Weapons Against Infectious Disease," *Contemporary Pediatrics*, October 2003. *Contemporary Pediatrics* is a copyrighted publication of Advanstar Communications, Inc. All rights reserved.

I n the course of a typical day in a pediatric office, dozens of prescriptions are written for antibiotics to treat a variety of routine
infections. Yet it was not so long ago, before antibiotics were
available, that pediatricians and other physicians were powerless
against infectious diseases. Our repertoire of treatments was
painfully limited to measures directed at reducing fever, encour-
aging hydration, and quarantining the sick to contain the spread
of life-threatening disease.

In little more than half a century, antibiotics have radically
changed the course of pediatric medicine. This review looks at the
impact of infectious disease on children in the preantibiotic era
and highlights the many serendipitous events that led to the discovery of pediatrics' most powerful therapeutic agents.

The Bad Old Days

When pediatrics was in its infancy in the last quarter of the 19th
century, children often died of diseases that are now preventable
with vaccines or easily treated with antibiotics. Typhoid and
cholera were common and marked by sporadic epidemics. Other
major causes of death in infants and children included diphtheria,
tuberculosis, scarlet fever, pertussis, meningitis, and pneumonia.

The 1850 United States census attributed more than 100,000
deaths to what were then called "miasmic diseases," including
cholera, typhoid fever, croup, scarlet fever, diphtheria, and whooping cough. Young children were most susceptible—more than half
of the deaths of children between 5 and 9 years of age were caused
by these diseases. As many as 70% of children who contracted
diphtheria died, and mortality from scarlet fever among children
under 2 years was 55% in 1840. Even as late as 1915, mortality
from scarlet fever among children under 5 years was around 30%.
(Some experts believe that the scarlet fever of this period was a
different disease, with a different etiology, than the illness we call
scarlet fever today.) The death rate from whooping cough ap-
proached 25% among infected children, and the disease killed
more than 10,000 children a year in the US as late as 1906.

Physicians used a variety of remedies to combat illness. Bloodletting was commonplace, as was the aggressive use of emetic and
cathartic agents. Bloodletting was achieved by using leeches or
lancing veins with nonsterile knives and applying heated cups to
the incision to encourage the free flow of blood. One of the most

common purgative agents was calomel, a preparation of mercuric chloride, which was given to children in high and frequent doses.

A prevailing belief at the time was that any measure that altered a patient's physiologic status combatted infection and could rid the body of toxins responsible for disease. For this reason, ill children were treated aggressively with sweating by placing them under dozens of blankets, or with "puking or purging," as mentioned. It was also believed that the human body could harbor only one illness at a time. Introducing a second infection—via an infected blister, for example—could "displace" an existing illness with one more likely to be survivable. Accordingly, children with serious illnesses were often treated by blistering of the skin with hot pokers, boiling water, or plasters containing acids.

As medicine evolved, so did novel treatments to combat infectious disease. Pertussis was treated by irradiating the chest with X-rays and, until the late 1800s, pharyngeal diphtheria was treated by injecting chlorine water into the diptheritic pseudomembrane or spraying the membrane with hydrogen peroxide. In 1885, a New York pediatrician, Joseph O'Dwyer, treated laryngeal diphtheria in children successfully by intubating the larynx with what became known as "O'Dwyer tubes." Eventually, as the bacterial basis of diphtheria came to be understood, this practice was replaced by the use of diphtheria antitoxin, which reduced mortality from diphtheria dramatically. The disease was subsequently conquered by the introduction of active immunization with toxin-antitoxin preparations.

The Germ Theory of Disease

Until the late 1800s, a time of enlightenment and transition for medicine, many different theories were advanced to explain the cause and spread of infectious disease. The Greeks introduced the concept that health resulted from the proper balance of four "humors"—blood, phlegm, yellow bile, and black bile—which led to the theory that bloodletting, emetics, and cathartics could bring the imbalance of humors that caused disease back into harmony. This idea persisted into the late 19th century. Later theories speculated that diseases resulted from the right (or wrong) combinations of climate, poor hygiene, and exposure to bad air.

The first theory that resembles our current understanding of disease transmission was formulated in 1546 by the Italian physician

Girolamo Fracastoro, who thought that disease was caused by invisible "particles" (translated into English as "germs"), which could spread through the air and produce illness by direct or indirect contact with human beings. It was not until 1683 that Antonie Van Leeuwenhoek, using a primitive microscope, demonstrated the existence of microorganisms, including protozoa and bacteria, and showed that they could be observed in the saliva and stool of humans and animals. He also discovered that the microorganisms he observed were fragile, and could be killed with vinegar or heat.

The first clinician to suspect that infection was spread from one person to another was Ignaz Semmelweis, a Hungarian physician. In 1847, he observed that the incidence of "childbed fever" in his Vienna Lying-in Hospital was dramatically lower among women whose babies were delivered by nurse midwives (3.9%) than those whose children were delivered by physicians (10%). He also noted that nurse midwives washed their hands between patients whereas physicians did not. He assumed that an agent responsible for infection—which he called "putrid particles"—was being transmitted by contact.

By implementing a policy of universal hand washing with lime chloride solution at the hospital, Semmelweiss drastically reduced the mortality of childbed fever to 1.27%. When he published his theories, however, few physicians believed him or adopted his recommendations. He remained a "medical martyr" until his practices were corroborated by later investigators who proved that bacteria were responsible for puerperal fever.

The next advances in the germ theory of disease came from two investigators in the late 19th century: Louis Pasteur, a French chemist, and Robert Koch, a German physician. Pasteur discovered that yeast was responsible for fermentation and that bacteria caused wine to spoil. By heating wine, and killing contaminating bacteria, he could prevent wine from spoiling. This discovery eventually led to wide-spread "pasteurization" of wine and was later adapted to prevent milk from spoiling.

Pasteur also discovered the microbial origin of anthrax, traced the causative organism's complicated life cycle, and determined that transmission could be avoided by burning, rather than burying, the corpses of infected animals. With his discovery that chickens could be protected from Vibrio cholerae infection by inoculation with old cultures of cholera bacteria, he laid the foundation for the process of attenuating bacteria to produce immunity. Pasteur's studies inspired Joseph Lister to disinfect operative wounds with carbolic acid to prevent postoperative wound infection, thereby introducing the concept of "antiseptic" surgery.

Whereas Pasteur pioneered the concept that bacteria were responsible for human disease, his rival Robert Koch was responsible for developing the modern science of microbiology. He perfected techniques for growing pure colonies of bacteria first on potato slices, then gelatin, then agar with enriched nutrients. He invented methods of fixing and staining bacteria and techniques for photographing the bacteria he viewed through his microscopes.

Koch demonstrated that specific bacteria were responsible for diseases including tuberculosis, cholera, anthrax, and many others. With his former professor, Jacob Henle, he formulated what have come to be known as the Henle-Koch postulates for proving that a specific organism is the causative agent of a particular disease:

• A specific organism must be identified in all cases of a disease
• Pure cultures of the organism must be obtained
• Organisms from pure culture must reproduce the disease in experimental animals
• The organism must be recovered from the experimental animals.

The Search for "Magic Bullets"

Once bacteria were understood to cause human diseases, the search began for agents that could kill infecting organisms while leaving the affected human unharmed. Some researchers focused on mobilizing the immune system to combat infection; others sought to develop chemical agents or "magic bullets" to eradicate microorganisms. The first approach met with success initially, leading to the use of passive immunity to fight infection and, eventually, to the development of vaccines to prevent many adult and pediatric diseases.

Two students of Robert Koch, Emil von Behring and Shibasabura Kitasato, isolated serum from animals injected with modified diphtheria bacteria and used the isolated antitoxin to treat a child with diphtheria successfully. The serum was produced commercially in 1892 and, in a short time, reduced mortality from diphtheria from 70% to 21%. In 1901, von Behring received the first Nobel Prize for medicine for his discovery of the first effective agent to treat infection.

In the first decade of the 20th century, Paul Ehrlich, a German physician, developed the first "magic bullet," a drug to treat syphilis. At that time, 10% of the adult male population of the US had syphilis, and congenital syphilis accounted for 1% of infant mortality. Before Ehrlich's discovery, the only treatment for syphilis was mercury, a poison that caused hair and tooth loss, mouth ulcers, and abdominal pain. Many patients considered the treatment worse than the disease.

Ehrlich began to search for chemicals capable of killing microbes in 1906, and his research eventually led him to investigate the antibacterial properties of an arsenic containing synthetic dye called atoxyl. In 1909, after 605 failed attempts to develop an effective drug from atoxyl, Ehrlich's 606th experiment with an atoxyl derivative, arsphenamine, succeeded. The compound was marketed in 1910 under the name of salvarsan and subsequently came into widespread use. In 1912, several American pediatricians . . . began to use salvarsan to treat infants with congenital syphilis.

The First Sulfa Drugs

With the success of salvarsan, the search for other "magic bullets" intensified, but the next antibiotic was not discovered for almost two decades. In 1932, Gerhard Domagk, a biochemist and the director of a German chemical company, began to experiment with textile dyes to see if any could effectively treat streptococcal infection. He discovered that a sulfa compound called Prontonsil cured mice that had been injected with a lethal dose of streptococci.

Shortly afterward, Domagk's daughter became violently ill with a streptococcal infection. When all other remedies failed her, Domagk administered Prontonsil, and she recovered rapidly and fully. One year later, Domagk published a clinical report describing how Prontonsil cured a 10-month-old child with staphylococcal septicemia. Studies subsequently showed that Prontonsil was effective in vivo, but not in vitro, because the body metabolized it into sulfanilamide, the agent that is active against bacteria. Still later, sulfa drugs were found to interfere with the metabolism of paraaminobenzoic acid, thereby stopping the growth of bacteria and exerting a bacteriostatic rather than a bacteriocidal effect.

Prontonsil was introduced into the US in 1935 to treat a child with *Haemophilus influenzae* meningitis at Babies Hospital in New York. Over the next several years, pharmaceutical companies produced many new sulfonamide antibiotics, including sulfapyridine and sulfadiazine. They proved more effective against pneumococcal infection than sulfanilamide, but were associated with nausea and kidney stones. Eventually, HoffmanLaRoche developed the soluble antibiotic sulfisoxazole, which became the most commonly prescribed sulfa drug.

In the early 1940s, huge quantities of sulfa drugs were prescribed in the US because they were found to be effective against pneumonia, meningitis, gonorrhea, and puerperal infection. When taken in a small dose daily, they reduced the recurrence of rheumatic fever. During World War II, American troops were given prophylactic doses of sulfa drugs to prevent streptococcal infection. Eventually, sulfa-resistant strains emerged.

In 1968, pediatricians began to prescribe a suspension of sulfamethoxazole and trimethoprim as an alternative to amoxicillin for otitis media and urinary tract infections. It is still a commonly used antibiotic for urinary tract infection.

The Discovery of Penicillin

The initial focus of antibiotic research was on synthetic chemicals with antimicrobial properties, but microbiologists next began to search for "natural" antibiotics. It had long been observed that one bacterial species inhibited the growth of others when introduced into the same culture medium. Researchers assumed that one species produced antibiotic substances that assured its survival at the expense of potential invaders.

The British physician and surgeon Alexander Fleming had gained limited notoriety in 1922 by discovering that tears and nasal secretions could inhibit the growth of bacteria. He subsequently identified and isolated the enzyme lysozyme from these secretions as well as from saliva, hair, and skin, and eggs, flowers, and vegetables. He speculated that lysozyme was a part of a universal defense mechanism that all living creatures possessed to prevent invasion by bacteria. Unfortunately, lysozyme had no effect on pathologic bacteria, and Fleming eventually abandoned research on the enzyme to study staphylococci.

Fortunately, Fleming was somewhat untidy in his laboratory. One day in 1928, he noticed that a mold (*Penicillium notatum*) that had contaminated old culture dishes in which staphylococci were growing produced a zone of inhibition where it grew. He later isolated a substance, which he called penicillin, from the mold and found that it effectively eradicated many different types of bacteria. He published his findings in 1929 but never attempted to administer penicillin to lab animals inoculated with bacteria.

Had it not been for other investigators at Oxford University in England who chanced upon Fleming's original paper, penicillin might never have been introduced as an antibiotic. The investigators—Howard Florey and Ernst Chain, a German Jew who had fled from Germany to England as Hitler rose to power—began to attempt to produce enough penicillin to determine its potential utility as an antibiotic. With the aid of a $5,000 grant from the Rockefeller Institute, Florey and Chain increased the yield of penicillin by growing P notatum in porcelain bedpans, and Chain produced small quantities of purified penicillin for testing. The penicillin he prepared was 1,000 times more potent than Fleming's original "mold juice extract" and appeared to have at least 10 times the antibiotic activity of sulfa drugs.

In a now-famous study published in the Lancet in 1940, Florey and Chain injected 50 mice with streptococci and treated half of them with penicillin. At the end of the experiment, all the untreated mice were dead; 24 of the 25 penicillin-treated mice survived.

One year later, Florey and Chain produced enough penicillin for a clinical test. The antibiotic was first administered to a policeman with streptococcal septicemia, who improved while receiving penicillin but eventually died once the penicillin supply was exhausted after five days of treatment. The next beneficiaries were children—a 15-year-old with hemolytic septicemia and a 4-year-old with cavernous-sinus thrombosis and sepsis. The 15-year-old survived; the 4-year-old died from a ruptured aneurysm after being cured of infection by the penicillin.

Unlike the sulfa drugs, which could be manufactured in quantity at reasonable expense, researchers labored for years to devise methods to produce useful quantities of penicillin. Florey and his associates left Britain for the US in 1941 because Britain could not allocate the resources Florey required to expand production while the country was at war. In the US, Florey and other researchers discovered that another fungus, *Penicillium chrysogenum*, produced twice as much penicillin as the original strains of *P notatum*—two units of penicillin for each milliliter of medium. When *P chrysogenum* was irradiated with ultraviolet light or X-rays, it could produce as much as 1,000 units of penicillin for each milliliter of medium. By 1944, more than 20 billion units of penicillin were being produced in the US, and production increased to more than 6,000 billion units the next year.

The first pediatrician to study the efficacy of penicillin in children was Roger L.J. Kennedy, who treated 54 children—with dramatic results. He used penicillin G, the first available therapeutic penicillin, which had to be administered intravenously or intramuscularly because gastric acid destroyed it rapidly when it was given orally. Within a few years, methods for manufacturing semisynthetic penicillins, which could withstand stomach acid and were effective when given orally, were developed. In 1953, penicillin V was prepared merely by adding phenoxyacetic acid to the growth medium.

In the years that followed, the pharmaceutical industry learned to modify penicillin by adding side chains of molecules. Ampicillin, introduced in 1961, was the first penicillin to have efficacy against gram-negative bacteria. Methicillin (1960), nafcillin (1961), and oxacillin (1962) were effective in treating infection caused by penicillinase-producing Staphylococcus species. Carbenicillin (1964) proved to be effective against Pseudomonas species. Amoxicillin, which could be given every eight hours, was introduced in 1969.

Antibiotics in Abundance

Following the success of penicillin, pharmaceutical researchers began to investigate a variety of fungi and bacteria to determine whether other useful antibiotics could be isolated. In 1945, Giuseppe Brotzu, an Italian researcher, isolated three cephalosporin compounds from the fungi Cephalosporium acremonium. It was not until 1964, however, that the first two therapeutic cephalosporins—cephalothin and cephaloridine—were introduced. They were effective against gram-positive and gram-negative bacteria and penicillin-resistant staphylococci. The first effective oral cephalosporin, cephalexin, was introduced in 1967. It was of limited use in children because the suspension tasted horrible and was not very effective in treating otitis media. Pediatricians would have to wait for an effective (and palatable) oral cephalosporin suspension until 1979, when Eli Lilly and Company marketed cefaclor. It rapidly became one of the most popular antibiotics for otitis media, strep pharyngitis, and skin and respiratory infections.

When the American microbiologist Selman Waksman—who is credited with inventing the word *antibiotic*—first studied the genus of soil bacteria *Actinomyces*, the result was several antibiotics that were too toxic for therapeutic use. In 1943, however, Waksman isolated streptomycin from *Streptomyces griseus*, an actinomycete. This first aminoglycoside antibiotic was found to be effective against tuberculosis. Other aminoglycosides soon followed. Neomycin was discovered in 1949; kanamycin, in 1957; and gentamicin, in 1963.

Many other actinomycetes were found to produce antibiotics as well. Chloramphenicol, derived from Streptomyces venequelae, was released in 1948 as one of the first broad-spectrum antibiotics with antirickettsial activity. It remained popular for decades but is used rarely today because of its association with aplastic anemia.

Tetracycline—derived from hydrogenolysis of chlortetracycline, which was produced from yet another actinomycete—became commercially available in the early 1950s. Doxycycline followed in 1966; minocycline, in 1972. Erythromycin, a macrolide antibiotic derived from Streptomyces erythreuse, was isolated in 1952, and vancomycin, a glycopeptide antibiotic derived from Streptomyces orientalis, was isolated in 1956. Today vancomycin is the drug of choice for treating methicillin-resistant Staphylococcus aureus infections.

In 1962, researchers identified nalidixic acid, a by-product of chloroquine synthesis, as being a potent "quinolone" antibiotic, but it was not until 1982 that fluorinated quinolone compounds, including ciprofloxacin, became available for general use. A new antibiotic of the oxazolindinone class, called linezolid, was recently approved by the FDA and should be available by the time you read this. Representing the first "new" antibiotic class in decades, linezolid was actually discovered more than 30 years ago but was never produced commercially. It is being introduced now because of the growing threat of antibiotic resistance.

The Bugs Strike Back

It was Alexander Fleming who first warned the medical community to use antibiotics cautiously. Overzealous, indiscriminate use would encourage the evolution of bacteria resistant to "magic bullets." His prediction came true not long after sulfa drugs and penicillin were introduced. By 1946, just three years after penicillin use became widespread, hospitals began reporting a rising occurrence of penicillin-resistant staphylococci. By the 1960s, penicillin-resistant pneumococci and gonococci were reported as well.

Penicillin was originally available without a prescription and was often used to treat nonbacterial infection, often in subtherapeutic doses. This undoubtedly contributed to the appearance of penicillin resistance.

Today, according to the Centers for Disease Control and Prevention (CDC), as many as 30% of infections caused by pneumoccoci are not susceptible to penicillin, and data gathered from intensive care units around the country indicate that 28% of nosocomial infections are resistant to the preferred antibiotic treatment. Most worrisome is the appearance of vancomycin-resistant strains of S aureus in Japan and the US since 1997.

To combat the evolving threat of antibiotic resistance, the CDC recently released a plan—Preventing Emerging Infectious Diseases: A Strategy for the 21st Century. The plan involves improving surveillance for drug-resistant infections, accelerating research that focuses on understanding antimicrobial resistance, developing infection control strategies to prevent disease transmission, developing new vaccines, and educating physicians to prescribe antibiotics more prudently. The Food and Drug Administration recently addressed the issue of drug resistance with a new rule for labeling antibiotics.

It is easy to forget the years of research and fortuitous events that have armed pediatricians with an arsenal of antibiotics to cure infections that were once life-threatening. Our obligation now is to preserve the efficacy of these drugs by adopting judicious prescribing habits. If we do that, we will have effective antibiotics for years to come.

Bringing Infectious Diseases Under Control

By the Centers for Disease Control and Prevention

The twentieth century has witnessed the golden age of microbiology and the decline of many infectious diseases. The discovery of microorganisms and founding of the germ theory of disease, as well as the improvement of sanitation and hygiene, prompted this decline of disease. The new fields of bacteriology and virology led to vaccines and antibiotics, as well as to new understandings about disease transmission—some microbes could be transmitted through the air, some by direct contact, and others only by blood. Advances in laboratory techniques also played a role. Serologic testing (using specific antibody-antigen reactions) was developed to diagnose diseases. Cell culture techniques were developed, which enable live viruses to be grown for vaccine development. Finally, the new field of molecular genetics has permitted the characterization of previously unknown disease agents. With all of these advances, the control of infectious disease is still a challenge. Complacency about "controlled" diseases has allowed many to resurface, and lack of global surveillance has allowed new diseases to spread. In 1999 the U.S. Centers for Disease Control and Prevention (CDC) published the following summary of the control of infectious diseases from 1900 to 1999.

D eaths from infectious diseases have declined markedly in the United States during the 20th century. This decline contributed to a sharp drop in infant and child mortality

Centers for Disease Control and Prevention, "Achievements in Public Health, 1900–1999: Control of Infectious Diseases," *Morbidity and Mortality Weekly Report*, July 30, 1999.

and to the 29.2-year increase in life expectancy. In 1900, 30.4% of all deaths occurred among children aged less than 5 years; in 1997, that percentage was only 1.4%. In 1900, the three leading causes of death were pneumonia, tuberculosis (TB), and diarrhea and enteritis, which (together with diphtheria) caused one third of all deaths. Of these deaths, 40% were among children aged less than 5 years. In 1997, heart disease and cancers accounted for 54.7% of all deaths, with 4.5% attributable to pneumonia, influenza, and human immunodeficiency virus (HIV) infection. Despite this overall progress, one of the most devastating epidemics in human history occurred during the 20th century: the 1918 influenza pandemic that resulted in 20 million deaths, including 500,000 in the United States, in less than 1 year—more than have died in as short a time during any war or famine in the world. HIV infection, first recognized in 1981, has caused a pandemic that is still in progress, affecting 33 million people and causing an estimated 13.9 million deaths. These episodes illustrate the volatility of infectious disease death rates and the unpredictability of disease emergence.

Public health action to control infectious diseases in the 20th century is based on the 19th-century discovery of microorganisms as the cause of many serious diseases (e.g., cholera and TB). Disease control resulted from improvements in sanitation and hygiene, the discovery of antibiotics, and the implementation of universal childhood vaccination programs. Scientific and technologic advances played a major role in each of these areas and are the foundation for today's disease surveillance and control systems. Scientific findings also have contributed to a new understanding of the evolving relation between humans and microbes.

Sanitation and Hygiene

The 19th-century shift in population from country to city that accompanied industrialization and immigration led to overcrowding in poor housing served by inadequate or nonexistent public water supplies and waste-disposal systems. These conditions resulted in repeated outbreaks of cholera, dysentery, TB, typhoid fever, influenza, yellow fever, and malaria.

By 1900, however, the incidence of many of these diseases had begun to decline because of public health improvements, implementation of which continued into the 20th century. Local, state, and federal efforts to improve sanitation and hygiene reinforced the concept of collective "public health" action (e.g., to prevent infection by providing clean drinking water). By 1900, 40 of the 45 states had established health departments. The first county health departments were established in 1908. From the 1930s through the 1950s, state and local health departments made substantial progress in disease prevention activities, including sewage disposal, water treatment, food safety, organized solid waste disposal, and public education about hygienic practices (e.g., foodhandling and handwashing). Chlorination and other treatments of drinking water began in the early 1900s and became widespread public health practices, further decreasing the incidence of waterborne diseases. The incidence of TB also declined as improvements in housing reduced crowding and TB-control programs were initiated. In 1900, 194 of every 100,000 U.S. residents died from TB; most were residents of urban areas. In 1940 (before the introduction of antibiotic therapy), TB remained a leading cause of death, but the crude death rate had decreased to 46 per 100,000 persons.

Animal and pest control also contributed to disease reduction. Nationally sponsored, state-coordinated vaccination and animal-control programs eliminated dog-to-dog transmission of rabies. Malaria, once endemic throughout the southeastern United States, was reduced to negligible levels by the late 1940s; regional mosquito-control programs played an important role in these efforts. Plague also diminished; the U.S. Marine Hospital Service (which later became the Public Health Service) led quarantine and ship inspection activities and rodent and vector-control operations. The last major rat-associated outbreak of plague in the United States occurred during 1924–1925 in Los Angeles. This outbreak included the last identified instance of human-to-human transmission of plague (through inhalation of infectious respiratory droplets from coughing patients) in this country.

Vaccination

Strategic vaccination campaigns have virtually eliminated diseases that previously were common in the United States, including diphtheria, tetanus, poliomyelitis, smallpox, measles, mumps, rubella, and *Haemophilus influenzae* type b meningitis. With the licensure of the combined diphtheria and tetanus toxoids and pertussis vaccine in 1949, state and local health departments instituted vaccination programs, aimed primarily at poor children. In 1955, the introduction of the Salk poliovirus vaccine led to federal funding of state and local childhood vaccination programs. In 1962, a federally coordinated vaccination program was established through the passage of the Vaccination Assistance Act—landmark legislation that has been renewed continuously and now supports the purchase and administration of a full range of childhood vaccines.

The success of vaccination programs in the United States and Europe inspired the 20th-century concept of "disease eradication"—the idea that a selected disease could be eradicated from all human populations through global cooperation. In 1977, after a decade-long campaign involving 33 nations, smallpox was eradicated worldwide—approximately a decade after it had been eliminated from the United States and the rest of the Western Hemisphere. Polio and dracunculiasis may be eradicated by 2000.

Antibiotics and Other Antimicrobial Medicines

Penicillin was developed into a widely available medical product that provided quick and complete treatment of previously incurable bacterial illnesses, with a wider range of targets and fewer side effects than sulfa drugs. Discovered fortuitously in 1928, penicillin was not developed for medical use until the 1940s, when it was produced in substantial quantities and used by the U.S. military to treat sick and wounded soldiers.

Antibiotics have been in civilian use for 57 years and have saved the lives of persons with streptococcal and staphylococcal infections, gonorrhea, syphilis, and other infections. Drugs also have been developed to treat viral diseases (e.g., herpes and HIV infection); fungal diseases (e.g., candidiasis and histoplasmosis); and parasitic diseases (e.g., malaria). . . . However, the emergence of drug resistance in many organisms is reversing some of the therapeutic miracles of the last 50 years and underscores the importance of disease prevention.

Technologic Advances in Detecting and Monitoring Infectious Diseases

Technologic changes that increased capacity for detecting, diagnosing, and monitoring infectious diseases included development early in the century of serologic testing and more recently the development of molecular assays based on nucleic acid and antibody probes. The use of computers and electronic forms of communication enhanced the ability to gather, analyze, and disseminate disease surveillance data.

Serologic testing came into use in the 1910s and has become a basic tool to diagnose and control many infectious diseases. Syphilis and gonorrhea, for example, were widespread early in the century and were difficult to diagnose, especially during the latent stages. The advent of serologic testing for syphilis helped provide a more accurate description of this public health problem and facilitated diagnosis of infection. For example, in New York City, serologic testing in 1901 indicated that 5%–19% of all men had syphilitic infections.

The first virus isolation techniques came into use at the turn of the century. They involved straining infected material through successively smaller sieves and inoculating test animals or plants to show the purified substance retained disease-causing activity. The first "filtered" viruses were tobacco mosaic virus (1882) and foot-and-mouth disease virus of cattle (1898). The U.S. Army Command under Walter Reed filtered yellow fever virus in 1900. The subsequent development of cell culture in the 1930s paved the way for large-scale production of live or heat-killed viral vaccines. Negative staining techniques for visualizing viruses under the electron microscope were available by the early 1960s.

During the last quarter of the 20th century, molecular biology has provided powerful new tools to detect and characterize infectious pathogens. The use of nucleic acid hybridization and sequencing techniques has made it possible to characterize the causative agents of previously unknown diseases (e.g., hepatitis C, human ehrlichiosis, hantavirus pulmonary syndrome, acquired immunodeficiency syndrome [AIDS], and Nipah virus disease).

Molecular tools have enhanced capacity to track the transmission of new threats and find new ways to prevent and treat them. Had AIDS emerged 100 years ago, when laboratory-based diagnostic methods were in their infancy, the disease might have remained a mysterious syndrome for many decades. Moreover, the drugs used to treat HIV-infected persons and prevent perinatal transmission (e.g., replication analogs and protease inhibitors) were developed based on a modern understanding of retroviral replication at the molecular level.

Challenges for the 21st Century

Success in reducing morbidity and mortality from infectious diseases during the first three quarters of the 20th century led to complacency about the need for continued research into treatment and control of infectious microbes. However, the appearance of AIDS, the re-emergence of TB (including multidrug-resistant strains), and an overall increase in infectious disease mortality during the 1980s and early 1990s provide additional evidence that as long as microbes can evolve, new diseases will appear. The emergence of new diseases underscores the importance of disease prevention through continual monitoring of underlying factors that may encourage the emergence or re-emergence of diseases.

Molecular genetics has provided a new appreciation of the remarkable ability of microbes to evolve, adapt, and develop drug resistance in an unpredictable and dynamic fashion. Resistance genes are transmitted from one bacterium to another on plasmids, and viruses evolve through replication errors and reassortment of gene segments and by jumping species barriers. Recent examples of microbial evolution include the emergence of a virulent strain of avian influenza in Hong Kong (1997–98); the multidrug-resistant W strain of *M. tuberculosis* in the United States in 1991, and *Staphylococcus aureus* with reduced susceptibility to vancomycin in Japan in 1996 and the United States in 1997.

For continued success in controlling infectious diseases, the U.S. public health system must prepare to address diverse challenges, including the emergence of new infectious diseases, the re-emergence of old diseases (sometimes in drug-resistant forms), large foodborne outbreaks, and acts of bioterrorism. Ongoing research on the possible role of infectious agents in causing or intensifying certain chronic diseases (including diabetes mellitus type 1, some cancers, and heart conditions) also is imperative. Continued protection of health requires improved capacity for disease surveillance and outbreak response at the local, state, federal, and global levels; the development and dissemination of new laboratory and epidemiologic methods; continued antimicrobial and vaccine development; and ongoing research into environmental factors that facilitate disease emergence.

CHAPTER 3

New Challenges

The Threat of Emerging Infectious Diseases

By Larry J. Strausbaugh

Larry J. Strausbaugh is a physician and epidemiologist (one who studies the cause and spread of disease in human populations) and a professor of medicine. He is also the project director for the Emerging Infections Network (EIN), a program cosponsored by the Centers for Disease Control and Prevention (CDC) and the Infectious Diseases Society of America (IDSA). The EIN serves to detect new or unusual clinical events, identify and track new cases of disease, collaborate with medical professionals about emerging diseases, and provide communication among professionals and to the public.

In 1997, Strausbaugh published an article to alert community physicians about emerging infectious diseases (EIDs). The term *EID* was coined in the 1990s, and it refers to any disease of infectious origin whose incidence has increased in the past two decades or threatens to increase in the future. These can be previously known or newly discovered diseases. In Strausbaugh's article, as excerpted here, he states that the modern world is faced with more than thirty new diseases since 1950, and more than fifteen resurgent diseases. Physician awareness and keen observation, as well as improved communication and surveillance within and between states and countries, will help researchers to identify and hopefully control these new and resurgent threats, Strausbaugh maintains.

T he terms "emerging infections" and "emerging infectious diseases" were initially brought to the attention of the medical community in 1992 in a report from the Institute of Medicine titled "Emerging Infections: Microbial Threats to Health in the

United States." The Centers for Disease Control and Prevention followed in 1994 with "Addressing Emerging Infectious Disease Threats: A Prevention Strategy for the United States." In January 1996, 36 journals in 21 countries agreed to devote all or part of an issue to emerging and reemerging global microbial threats. . . . The concept of emerging infections arose from national and global concerns about public health. Nevertheless, the concept has ramifications for physicians in every kind of practice situation, especially those who provide primary care.

The Concept of Emerging Infectious Diseases

The Institute of Medicine and the CDC have defined emerging infections as diseases of infectious origin with an incidence that has increased within the past two decades or threatens to increase in the near future. In many cases, the microbial cause of the disease was discovered only within the past two decades (Table 1). The hantavirus pulmonary syndrome caused by the Sin Nombre virus, which was discovered in 1993, is a recent example. Although many of the clinical conditions listed in Table 1 were recognized before the isolation of their causative agents, new information on incidence, prevalence and geographic distribution has qualified them for inclusion as an emerging infection.

Table 1
Some Microbial Agents and Associated Disease Identified Since 1975

Year	Microbe	Diseases
1975	Parvovirus B19	Fifth disease; aplastic crisis in chronic hemolytic anemia
1976	Cryptosporidium parvum	Enterocolitis
1977	Ebola virus	Ebola hemorrhagic fever
1977	Legionella pneumophila	Legionnaires disease
1977	Campylobacter species	Enterocolitis
1981	Toxin-producing strains of Staphylococcus aureus	Toxic shock syndrome
1982	Escherichia coli 0157:E7	Hemorrhagic colitis; hemolytic uremia syndrome
1982	Borrelia burgdorferi	Lyme disease

1983	Human immunodeficiency virus	Acquired immunodeficiency syndrome
1983	Helicobacter pylori	Duodenal and gastric ulcers
1988	Human herpesvirus-6	Roseola subitum
1989	Ehrlichia chaffeensis	Human ehrlichiosis
1989	Hepatitis C virus	Parenterally transmitted non-A, non-B hepatitis
1992	Bartonella henselae	Cat-scratch disease; bacillary angiomatosis
1993	Sin Nombre virus	Hantavirus pulmonary

The other category of emerging infectious diseases involves known pathogens that are reemerging at a specific time and in a specific place (Table 2). The outbreaks of plague in India during 1994 and the outbreak of meningococcal disease in Oregon since 1994 are examples of this type of emerging infection. The outbreak of meningococcal disease in Oregon was importation of a new strain of Neisseria meningitidis type B, designated ET-5, that had previously caused outbreaks in Scandinavia, Cuba and Chile.

Table 2

Examples of Resurgent Emerging Infections in 1990s

Year	Place	Resurgent infectious disease
1995	Zaire	Ebola hemorrhagic fever
1994	India	Plague
1994–96	Oregon	Meningococcal disease
1993	Wisconsin	Cryptosporidiosis
1992–96	United States	Vancomycin-resistant enterococci infections
1993–96	United States	Penicillin-resistant pneumococcol infections
1989–96	United States	Streptococcol toxic shock syndrome
1993	Ohio	Pertussis
1992	California	Coccidioidomycosis
1990	New York	Multidrug-resistant tuberculosis

The concept of emerging infections is flexible, reflecting not only the temporal and geographic interactions between humans and microbes, but also the ability of the medical community to identify them. The relationship between man and microbe is seldom stable. New threats are ever present, confronting public health authorities as well as physicians.

In its 1992 report, the Institute of Medicine listed six factors that have accounted for the increased incidence of certain infections during the past two decades. These factors and specific examples for each are listed in Table 3.

Table 3
Factors Responsibities for Emerging Infectious Diseases and Specific Examples

Factors	Examples
Changes in human demographics and behavior	Sexual revolution and incidence of sexually transmitted diseases; immunosuppression and fungal infections
Changes in technology and industry	Modern medical care and nosocomial infections; antimicrobial supplemented animal feeds and resistant salmonellae
Economic development and land use	Dam building and Rift Valley Fever in eastern Africa; reforestation and Lyme disease in the northeastern United States
International travel and commerce	Malaria in the United States; cholera in North and South America
Microbial adaptation and change	Antimicrobial resistant pathogens; influenza pandemics
Breakdown of public health measure	Measles in the United States; diphtheria in Russia

Recognition of Emerging Infectious Diseases

Recognition of emerging infectious diseases begins with a knowledge of the new entities themselves, especially their clinical features, epidemiology and diagnosis. Knowledge of disease trends and of regional or community experience with emerging infections is also helpful and may be sought from colleagues, regional meetings or publications from local health departments. With this knowledge, physicians will be prepared to consider the diagnosis of an emerging infection when the clinical features and epidemiologic setting suggest something out of the ordinary. At times, such recognition may be as easy as reading an antimicrobial susceptibility report. At other times, a physician may be faced with a completely new condition (e.g., ehrlichiosis). In such situations, consultation with a clinical microbiologist, pathologist, infectious disease specialist or public health authority is often helpful to discern the optimal diagnostic strategy (i.e., what the most precise diagnostic test is and where it is available).

Practicing physicians may also encounter new entities that have not yet been identified or adequately described. Recognizing these novel conditions is surely one of the greatest challenges in medicine, and often the astute observations of practicing physicians are the first step in the discovery process. Certain findings can prompt consideration of a new type of infection. Clusters of febrile illnesses with similar clinical features, especially unusual features like bloody diarrhea or respiratory failure, that do not conform to those of known entities, may raise suspicions. Similarly, severe or fatal febrile illnesses without a diagnosis in otherwise healthy persons may stimulate consideration of new or resurgent agents. Last, unusual environmental exposures present in undiagnosed febrile illness may raise concern. Insect or rodent exposure in the history, for example, may provide important clues to the presence of a new agent.

Response to Emerging Infectious Diseases

After recognizing the presence of an emerging infectious disease, physicians have three additional obligations. First, they must secure appropriate therapy for their patient and manage their case with an eye toward possible complications. Second, they must consider the risk to those who have been in contact with the infected patient and decide whether prophylaxis, isolation or other actions are indicated. Last, physicians caring for patients with an emerging infection need to notify local public health authorities. In some states, notification is mandated by law for certain infections. In other situations, notification is voluntary but is appreciated because it provides an opportunity for in-depth investigation and widespread dissemination of information to other physicians and health care providers in the area.

The Debate over the Prion

By Steve Mitchell

Journalist Steve Mitchell has been writing about science and medicine for over eight years. He has written about WebMD, Reuters Health, the Food and Drug Administration, the National Institutes of Health, and other medical organizations, as well as contributed to scientific journals, including the *Lancet*. As the current medical correspondent for United Press International (UPI), he wrote the following article about prion research. *Prion*, which stands for proteinaceous infectious agent, is a term that was coined by American neurologist Stanley B. Prusiner in the 1980s. Prusiner studies transmissible spongiform encephalopathies (TSEs), fatal human and animal neurodegenerative diseases such as scrapie, mad cow, and chronic wasting disease in animals and Kuru, Creutzfeldt-Jakob disease (CJD), and variant CJD (vCJD) in humans. He hypothesized that the infectious agent for these diseases is actually just a misshaped form of a normal protein that is found in all tissues. He called this unusual protein a prion. The misshaped proteins, or prions, cause the normal proteins to convert to the abnormal shape, and the resulting accumulation of these abnormal proteins causes neurologic damage and ultimately death. If Prusiner is correct, then prions are a new type of infectious agent. In the 1980s the scientific community was skeptical about Prusiner's hypothesis; however, in the past decade, the media and much of the scientific world has begun to work the prion hypothesis as fact. Mitchell points out, however, that the hypothesis has still not been proven and that some researchers think money and time is being misdirected. Many companies and laboratories are trying to develop prion disinfection techniques and prion treatments, while few seem to be trying to determine with certainty the infectious cause of these diseases.

Millions of federal dollars being spent to find treatments and diagnostics for mad cow disease and similar brain disorders in humans might be misguided and actually delaying the development of effective medications that could cure or prevent these deadly disorders, experts have told United Press International (UPI).

Although prions, as the suspicious proteins are called, generally have been accepted as the pathogens that cause mad cow disease and its human equivalent, variant Creutzfeldt-Jakob disease (vCJD), so far investigators have been unsuccessful at demonstrating the agents are infectious. This leaves open the possibility, as a growing body of research suggests, the diseases are caused by some other pathogen—possibly a virus or bacteria.

The National Institutes of Health (NIH) in Bethesda, Maryland, openly acknowledges prions have not been established fully as a cause of any disease. Yet nearly all of the $27 million the agency doled out [in 2003] for studies on transmissible spongiform encephalopathies, or TSEs—a group of diseases that includes mad cow, chronic wasting in deer and elk, scrapie in sheep and vCJD in humans—went toward studies focusing on the prion hypothesis. Little of the money has been slated for research examining alternative causes of the disorders. In addition, the NIH has handed out $9 million to private companies for five-year contracts to develop blood-based tests for prions.

TSEs, so named because they "eat" holes in the brain, yielding a sponge-like appearance, have no treatment and are always fatal. Infected patients develop mental deterioration and physical incoordination that progresses to dementia and they often die within months.

Prions Have Not Been Proven Infectious

Prions are proteins normally found in the body. Their function remains uncertain, but in some cases they can malfunction. Proteins fold into 3-D shapes, but prions sometimes can misfold and assume incorrect shapes. The current hypothesis holds abnormal prions are infectious and cause the brain destruction seen in TSEs. Some experts insist, however, there is scant scientific evidence to support this.

"The best-kept secret in this field is that (prions) in any form have never shown infectivity," said Laura Manuelidis, head of the neuropathology section at Yale University's surgery department in New Haven, Connecticut.

Most researchers working in this field "know the data just aren't there" to support the hypothesis prions are the cause, Manuelidis told UPI. She has pointed out the lack of evidence supporting the role prions play in causing TSEs since the idea first was proposed in the 1980s.

Some researchers in this field think the mutant prions are the result—not the cause—of the disorders. These dissenting scientists theorize some other, as-yet-unidentified pathogen, such as bacteria or a virus, causes prions to misfold, which is what damages the brain. But they said it is nearly impossible to obtain funding to investigate alternative causes of TSEs.

The divergent theories represent a major medical research problem: If the prion concept turns out to be wrong, current efforts to find diagnostics and treatments for TSEs could be wasting both time and money.

Screening for Prions

The potential problem extends far beyond the research community, however. The recent discovery of a cow in Washington state infected with mad cow disease shows how TSEs could be making their way into the U.S. food supply. Other cases could go undetected because current mad-cow screening methods are based on detecting abnormal prions—which show up in advanced stages of the disease but do not seem to be present in the early stages.

Some animals that die might never show any evidence of misfolded proteins, said Frank Began of Tulane University in New Orleans, who thinks the disorder is caused by a bacteria. He recently presented evidence backing up his claim at a national scientific meeting in 2003.

This means if a virus or bacteria does cause the disorder, then current tests might never pick up animals that are infected but do not yet have symptoms.

Even if the prion hypothesis is correct, the millions of dollars being spent on that type of research should have led to a treatment by now, Bastian said. "Why don't we have it solved?" he asked. "I believe we're going in the wrong direction."

The race to find treatments for TSEs has generated urgency in recent years because of a mad cow outbreak in the United Kingdom that crossed over into humans in the mid-1990s, infecting more than 100 people with vCJD. Since then, 22 other countries have detected the disease in their cattle—including the United States and Canada, which reported their first domestic cases [in 2003].

Along with the first U.S. case of mad cow, the country is experiencing a growing outbreak of a similar disorder called chronic wasting disease in deer and elk in the Midwest and West, and there are concerns this could be transmitted to cattle and humans.

Other countries—even those that have experienced mad cow outbreaks—also have failed to fund research proposing alternative ideas, according to Heino Diringer, a retired biochemist who was affiliated with the Robert Koch Institute in Berlin. He also doubts the prion hypothesis.

"Who's looking for (alternative causes) in Germany?" Diringer asked. "Nobody. In England? Only (one) group in Edinborough. But if researchers apply for looking for the agent there's no money because the agent has been discovered, according to the Nobel prize committee."

This is a problem. Diringer said, because "it will turn out that the prion concept is wrong."

Biased Funding of Research

The NIH—the agency responsible for dispensing U.S. federal research funds for diseases ranging from TSEs to cancer—acknowledges prions have not been shown conclusively to be the agent that causes TSEs. Some researchers consider the prion hypothesis unproven.

"Formally, I agree with them," said Chris Beisel, the National Institute of Allergy and Infectious Diseases (NIAID) program officer who funds prion research. He said NIAID is not funding many studies looking at alternative causes because few researchers are proposing this type of inquiry.

"I'm not aware of anyone who desperately wants to address this issue who has been turned away for funding," Beisel told UPI. "The money is there if somebody puts in a good application."

One factor holding up funding is the quality of the research being proposed, Beisel said.

"It's not that the individuals (in charge of funding) are averse to totally dumping existing dogma, but if you're going to challenge something, they don't want to throw a lot of money at something that isn't likely to produce good results. They want to see good solid experiments that are well-controlled (and) that are going to produce a definitive answer, one way or the other."

Several researchers, including an NIH scientist, claimed the research community is not applying for grants because there is a perception of bias—pursuing funding for alternative hypotheses is futile because such applications will be rejected.

"A lot of people have given up on (doing research to look for alternative causes) because they have been unable to get funding," said the NIH scientist, who requested anonymity and who doubts prions are the primary cause of TSEs.

Stanley Prusiner and the Prion Hypothesis

The idea prions cause mad cow disease, CJD and other similar deadly illnesses got its start in the early 1980s. Although the scientific community initially attacked the idea as invalid, the concept gained steam until it generally was accepted by most working in the field.

Dr. Stanley Prusiner, of the University of California, San Francisco, who first proposed the prion hypothesis, won the Nobel prize for his work in 1997. Since then and even several years before, NIH funding into mad cow and similar diseases has focused primarily on the prion concept, ignoring alternative causes.

A survey done by *Science* magazine found Prusiner's lab ranked first among all those receiving NIH funding in 2001. That year Prusiner's lab received some $12.5 million, several million dollars more than the next-highest-funded project.

Prusiner's lab even received more money than any single facility working on AIDS, cancer or heart disease and he continues to be heavily funded by the agency for his projects to develop diagnostic tests for TSEs based on detecting abnormal prions.

Dr. Jiri Safar, an associate professor working in Prusiner's lab, defended the prion concept and said although prions have not been proven to be infectious, several other lines of evidence indicate the misfolded prions are the cause of TSEs. So it becomes illogical to think something else may be the cause, he said.

Safar conceded "theoretically" that dissenting scientists "may actually be correct" and TSEs are caused by some other pathogen. If so, he said, they need to prove their hypotheses. Long before the prion theory was proposed, he noted, scientists had searched, unsuccessfully, for a virus that might be the cause of TSEs.

Reluctance to Propose Alternative Research

Other NIH agencies also are not funding many non-prion studies. The National Institute of Neurological Disorders and Stroke (NINDS) doled out more than $14 million to study TSEs in 2002, but nearly all of the money went to research focused on prions.

NINDS officials maintain they are open to proposals to investigate alternative causes of TSEs, but like the NIAID, the agency has received few applications proposing such research. Even if the number of proposals increased, a procedural limitation skews how NINDS could approve research into alternative causes of TSEs. The bulk of the proposals received focus on the prion theory and because it can fund only about 23 percent of those applications, nearly all of the research grants go for prion studies.

A second researcher who requested anonymity said no scientist would waste the time to apply for grants to study alternative causes of TSEs. . . .

Prion Research Is Worthwhile

Safar said much still is not known about prions, so more research should be conducted on the basic mechanism of infection in TSEs. "We can learn a lot, not only about the prions but also about other diseases caused by malfunctioning proteins," such as Alzheimer's and Parkinson's, he said.

Learning more about the basic biology of prions also could help uncover targets that medications could attack, he added.

Safar noted studies about the basic biology of the human immunodeficiency virus helped pave the way for more effective medications to fight AIDS and they continue to help researchers design vaccines that one day might be used to prevent infection. Prion research might do the same for TSEs.

One of the biggest mysteries of prions is how an agent that lacks DNA and RNA—used by all other living organisms to reproduce—makes copies of itself and amplifies itself in the brains of those it infects. Also, it remains unclear how prions destroy brain tissue.

As Safar put it, "We are essentially shooting in the dark."

Yet NINDS officials said they are not concerned hindering funding into alternative causes of TSEs could delay therapies. Michael Nunn, the agency's program director, said NINDS relies on researchers in the TSEs field to help determine the validity of the prion concept. He said many of these researchers will spend their entire careers in this field and therefore they would not want to waste their time. So they spend a lot of time thinking about the possibility of alternative causes of TSEs. . . .

Prion Researchers Have Strong Influence

Manuelidis and her colleagues have tried repeatedly to make known their doubts about prions, but so far their comments have fallen on deaf ears. She said she thinks the problem is not the NIH but the general scientific community working in this field. Top journals only are interested in publishing papers about prions, not alternative ideas, she said, and this in turn spills over into the smaller journals, creating an atmosphere that accepts only prions as the possible cause of TSEs.

When negative findings are published about prions, researchers often do not acknowledge the possibility prions might not be infectious—as is done with other infectious diseases—and younger researchers have been so inundated with the prion concept they tend not to stop and examine the evidence for themselves.

In addition, the big names in this field stand by the prion concept. These scientists tend to receive the most funds and are revered by journals and scientific organizations, so they are able to exert enormous influence over the rest of the field, Manuelidis said.

A Possible Viral Cause

One problem with pinpointing prions as the cause of TSEs is it is very difficult to isolate them. Laboratory preparations also contain other things, which could include unidentified bacteria or viruses. Therefore, even if the sample appears to infect animals and cause the disease, it is impossible to be sure prions are the cause, not other substances found in the preparation.

Manuelidis said she thinks current evidence suggests a virus as the culpable agent. She has shown sterilization procedures that should kill viruses can reduce infectivity of prion-containing preparations by 99.9 percent. Yet the prions, which are very resistant to sterilization techniques, are not damaged. This indicates the causative agent is an as-yet-unidentified virus, she explained.

This view is shared by the NIH researcher who noted that by itself an abnormal prion does not appear to be infectious or cause disease.

"So something is missing and one possibility is that what's missing is a virus," the NIH researcher said.

One plausible mechanism is the virus interacts with normal prions and causes them to assume an abnormal shape, which is how TSE diseases damage brain cells.

The virus theory would help explain why only certain individuals become ill with these diseases. Not all mice with mutated prions fall ill. It also could be having abnormal prions makes people vulnerable to infection with the virus, the NIH scientist speculated.

Prions Do Play a Role in TSEs

Manuelidis and the NIH researcher conceded, however, efforts to develop treatments based on prions might not be entirely futile because the abnormally folded proteins appear to play some role in the diseases. Safar pointed out antibodies and other agents that block prions have had some success in stopping the progression of TSEs.

That also means the prion-based diagnostic tests being developed also might be useful because detecting misfolded prions does indicate the presence of the diseases. Still, if they are caused by a virus or bacteria, being able to find the infectious organism would enable faster detection of the diseases and, if a treatment is developed, initiation of medication before the brain is damaged.

Safar's group is developing a test that can detect the disease soon after infection. Early detection is critical because if the disease is not detected until advanced stages, it is too late to prevent or reverse the brain destruction, he said.

A Possible Bacterial Cause

One alternative idea that has received NINDS funding is a small project by Bastian. He has uncovered evidence a bacteria could play a role in causing TSEs. The grant is only $185,000, however, a far cry from the millions heaped upon researchers focusing on the prion concept.

Yet Bastian has made progress. He presented research at the American Association of Neuropathology meeting in Orlando in June showing DNA from a type of bacteria carried by many insect species—spiralplasma—can be found in brains of people with CJD and in sheep brains infected with scrapie. The bacteria cannot be found in normal, healthy brains.

The bacteria, found in ticks and mosquitoes, also have been shown to cause a type of spongiform disease in rats and mice, Bastian said.

"There's really clear evidence that there's an association of the bacteria with this disease," he said.

He said he suspects the bacteria could cause prions to mutate and fold abnormally, and this could cause the brain destruction.

To Bastian, the idea that bacteria carried by insects cause these diseases fits with what currently is known about how they are transmitted. One unexplainable phenomenon about scrapie in sheep is the animals can catch the disease without having contact with infected individuals. To explain this, some researchers have proposed the disease can arise spontaneously. However, sheep in New Zealand display no evidence of the disease—yet they should have experienced at least a few cases if it arises spontaneously.

If TSEs are transmitted by insects, Bastian explained, and if the insects in New Zealand do not carry the bacteria, this would explain why sheep in that island country are free of the disease. The insect/bacteria hypothesis also fits with the pattern of bouts of chronic wasting disease seen in deer and elk in the Midwestern and western United States. Animal researchers there have been baffled by the disease, which appears to jump from herd to herd even though the animals do not come into contact with one another.

The Next Flu Pandemic

By Richard J. Webby and Robert G. Webster

Virologists Richard J. Webby and Robert G. Webster both work in the Department of Infectious Diseases at St. Jude Children's Research Hospital in Memphis, Tennessee. Dr. Webby heads a collaborative research project to study Influenza A (bird flu), and Dr. Webster has published over four hundred original virology articles and received the Bristol-Myers Squibb Infectious Diseases Award for work in understanding and controlling epidemic influenza virus. In 2003, they published the following article presenting the influenza epidemics of the past one hundred years and outlining the challenges for facing the next influenza pandemic, which they believe to be imminent.

The number of new strains of influenza viruses that can infect humans have been increasing, the authors state, and the next strain that can be transmitted from human to human could be catastrophic for the world population. Due to the number of animal reservoirs and the ability of the flu virus to continually change, a new flu vaccine must be produced every year. Even then, the vaccine is just a guess at what exact strains will cause trouble during the next flu season. If a new, highly virulent, human strain appeared, the authors suggest that the world would not be ready to handle it. According to Webby and Webster, the emergency preparedness for a flu pandemic is weak. Vaccine development and production are currently limited, time-consuming, and bogged down with potential liabilities; and, countries have not stored antiviral drugs to alleviate patients during an epidemic while vaccines are made.

I n February 2003, during a family visit to mainland China, a young girl from Hong Kong died of an unidentified respiratory illness. After returning to Hong Kong, both her father and brother were hospitalized with severe respiratory disease, which proved fatal to the father. When H5N1 (avian) influenza virus was isolated from both patients, the World Health Organization (WHO) went to pandemic alert status. At about the same time, there were rumors of rampant influenza-like disease in China. Influenza experts feared that H5N1 influenza virus had acquired the ominous capacity to pass from human to human. That outbreak is now known to have been SARS (severe acute respiratory syndrome), caused by a novel coronavirus.

In March 2003, another alarming situation arose on the other side of the world. A highly pathogenic H7N7 avian influenza outbreak had recently erupted in the poultry industry of the Netherlands, and workers involved in the slaughter of infected flocks contracted viral conjunctivitis. The H7N7 virus isolated from these patients had several disquieting features: Not only could it replicate in the human conjunctiva, but there was also evidence of human-to-human spread. Nearby herds of swine (which are often implicated in the adaptation of influenza viruses to humans) also showed serologic evidence of exposure. When a veterinarian died of respiratory infection, WHO again acknowledged the presence of a severe threat.

Luckily, the worst-case scenarios did not come about in either of the 2003 avian influenza virus scares. However, the year's events eliminated any remaining doubts that global advance planning for pandemic influenza is necessary. They also highlighted how far, as a scientific community, we have come since the [first documented avian-to-human influenza transmission in] 1997: We are now much better equipped with technologies and reagents to rapidly identify and respond to pandemic influenza threats. On the other hand, the legislative and infrastructure changes needed to translate these advances into real public health benefits are alarmingly slow.

The Role of WHO in Influenza Surveillance and Control

In 2001, WHO initiated the development of a Global Agenda for Influenza Surveillance and Control. Its four main objectives are to strengthen influenza surveillance, improve knowledge of the disease burden, increase vaccine use, and accelerate pandemic preparedness. In May 2002, this document was adopted after proposals and public comment were invited. The document advocates the development of methods and reagents that can be used to rapidly identify all influenza virus subtypes, thereby allowing integrated influenza surveillance in humans and in other animals. WHO, with its global influenza network of more than 100 laboratories and its distinguished record of planning for yearly interpandemic influenza, is ideally situated to play a broader role in facilitating international cooperation for the rapid exchange of viruses, reagents, and information. Influenza continually evolves at the human–lower animal interface and thus can be unpredictable. As an example, within a brief period, the H7N7 virus events occurred in European poultry and humans, H5N1 viruses infected Asian poultry and humans, and novel, rapidly spreading reassortant viruses were isolated in swine in the United States. Therefore, the capacity to simultaneously manage multiple potential pandemic situations is important. The WHO global agenda document will help to prioritize areas of influenza research and facilitate national pandemic preparedness plans.

Prioritization of Viral Subtypes for Surveillance and Control

Influenza experts agree that another influenza pandemic is inevitable and may be imminent. A major challenge in controlling influenza is the sheer magnitude of the animal reservoirs. It is not logistically possible to prepare reagents and vaccines against all strains of influenza encountered in animal reservoirs, and therefore, virus subtypes must be prioritized for pandemic vaccine and reagent preparation. Preliminary findings have identified the H2, H5, H6, H7, and H9 subtypes of influenza A as those most likely to be transmitted to humans. [Influenza viruses are typed according to their hemagglutinin (H) and neuraminidase (N) surface glycoproteins.] The influenza A subtypes currently circulating in humans, H1 and H3, continue to experience antigenic drift. That is, their antigenic surface glycoproteins are continually modified, allowing them to escape the population's immunity to the previous strain and thus to continue causing annual outbreaks. Although these continual modifications may lead to an increase in virulence, the mildness of the past three influenza seasons suggests that the dominance of the H1N1 and H3N2 viruses is waning as their ability to cause serious disease becomes increasingly attenuated. H2 influenza viruses are included in the high-risk category because they were the causative agent of the 1957 "Asian flu" pandemic and were the only influenza A subtype circulating in humans between 1957 and 1968. Counterparts of the 1957 H2N2 pandemic virus continue to circulate in wild and domestic duck reservoirs. Under the right conditions (which are still not completely understood), H2N2 viruses could again be transmitted to and spread among humans, none of whom under the age of 30 years now has immunity to this virus. Seroarchaeology data from the late 19th and early 20th centuries indicate that only the H1, H2, and H3 influenza virus subtypes have been successfully transmitted among humans. It is possible, but unlikely, that they are the only subtypes able to do so.

Not only are the H1, H2, and H3 influenza viruses of concern, but the H5 subtype has threatened to emerge as a human pandemic pathogen since 1997, when it killed 6 of 18 infected humans. Before that event, the receptor specificity of avian influenza viruses was thought to prevent their direct transmission to humans. Transmission from aquatic birds to humans was hypothesized to require infection of an intermediate host, such as the pig, that has both human-specific ($\propto$2-6 sialic acid) and avian-specific ($\propto$2-3 sialic acid) receptors on its respiratory epithelium. The 1997 H5N1 event demonstrated that domestic poultry species may also act as intermediate hosts. H5N1 viruses continue to emerge and evolve despite heroic measures taken to break their evolutionary cycle in the live poultry markets of Hong Kong: the elimination of live ducks and geese (the original source), the elimination of quail (the source of the internal genes of H5N1/97), and the institution of monthly "clean days," when all 1000-plus retail markets are emptied and cleaned.

Two things have become clear. Live poultry markets are potential breeding grounds for influenza and other emerging disease agents, and there is an Asian source of H5N1 influenza viruses outside of Hong Kong SAR. Between 1997 and 2003, H5N1 virus was isolated from duck meat imported from China into Korea and Japan. These observations suggest that ducks and possibly other avian species in mainland China are a reservoir of H5N1, although there have been no official reports of H5N1 virus in China.

At the beginning of the SARS outbreak, China missed an opportunity to show the world its considerable intellectual and scientific potential. In the case of H5N1 influenza, a pandemic in waiting, it remains to be seen whether China will show leadership in proactively addressing the problem. Concerted national and international efforts are required to deal effectively with the threat.

The third virus subtype on the most wanted list is H7. The H7 and H5 viruses have a unique ability to evolve into a form highly virulent to chickens and turkeys by acquiring additional amino acids at the hemagglutinin (HA) cleavage site (HA cleavage is required for viral infectivity). The highly pathogenic H7N7 influenza viruses that were lethal to poultry infected the eyes of more than 80 humans and killed one person. In the case of this outbreak, the Netherlands' policy of openness was important in reducing the potential threat and should serve as a model. When the virus was first detected at the end of February 2003, the European Community and international community, via the Office International des Epizooties, were notified so that surrounding countries, including Belgium and Germany, could immediately respond if the disease was detected. Culling of all poultry on infected farms and quarantine of surrounding farms succeeded in eradicating the virus once the etiologic agent was identified. After human infection was observed, an anti-influenza drug was given as prophylaxis, and vaccination with the current human influenza vaccine was done to reduce the likelihood that the avian virus would reassort with human H1N1 and H3N2 strains.

The remaining two viral subtypes on the priority list, H6 and H9, do not share the virulent phenotypes of the H5 and H7 viruses, but still pose a considerable threat. Both of these influenza viruses have spread from a wild aquatic bird reservoir to domestic poultry over the past 10 years. H9N2 viruses have also been detected in humans and in pigs and have acquired human-like receptor specificity. Neither of these viruses was able to infect chickens before the mid-1980s. Now, for unknown reasons, H9 viruses are endemic in chickens in Eurasia and H6 viruses are becoming endemic in both Eurasia and the Americas. These facts highlight the continuing adaptation of influenza viruses in the aquatic bird reservoirs to domestic chickens.

The Challenge of Developing Candidate Vaccines

If the next influenza pandemic were to begin tomorrow, inactivated vaccines would offer the only immediate means of mass prophylaxis, yet their supply is limited by inadequate production capabilities and suboptimal utilization of adjuvants. The stocks of antiviral drugs are too low to cope with an epidemic and would be quickly depleted. Tissue culture–based and live attenuated vaccines are now licensed in some countries, and could supplement the supply of inactivated vaccine. Further development of these options is urgently needed to provide alternative substrates in the face of a pandemic.

Since the 1970s, influenza vaccines have been made by exploiting the tendency of the segmented influenza genome to reassort. This natural process has been used to produce vaccine strains that simultaneously contain gene segments that allow them to grow well in eggs and gene segments that produce the desired antigenicity. Natural reassortment is allowed to occur in embryonated chicken eggs, and reassortants with the desired characteristics are selected. . . . Although this process creates an effective and safe influenza vaccine, it is too time-consuming and too dependent on a steady supply of eggs to be reliable in the face of a pandemic emergency. Even during interpandemic periods, 6 months is required to organize sufficient fertile chicken eggs for annual vaccine manufacture, and the preparation of the desired recombinant vaccine strain can be a time-consuming process. Influenza vaccine preparation is seasonal and is a remarkable achievement, in that an essentially new vaccine is made every year. However, two of the viruses of greatest concern, those of the highly pathogenic H5 and H7 subtypes, cannot be successfully grown in eggs. . . .

The most promising means of expediting the response to pandemic influenza is the use of plasmid-based reverse genetic systems to construct influenza virions and vaccines. These systems also offer a successful alternative means of producing H5 and H7 vaccine seed strains. . . . The next step is to take these plasmid-derived influenza vaccines through clinical trials to address crucial questions such as number and quantity of doses and the role of adjuvants. Most of the vaccines derived after the 1997 H5N1 episode by various alternative strategies induced a disappointing immune response. The optimal pandemic vaccination regimens can be anticipated only by collecting the necessary data and experience through clinical trials of vaccines against different subtypes of influenza virus.

Although they are well suited to the manufacture of inactivated influenza vaccines, reverse genetic systems introduce new variables. One of the most limiting of these is the need to use cell lines. There are surprisingly few suitable accredited cell lines and cell banks available, and many of those are the property of pharmaceutical companies. The practical options are very few, in view of the technical and regulatory restrictions. Perhaps the only cell line that meets all criteria for international use at this time is the African green monkey kidney cell line, Vero. However, although Vero cell lines are in widespread laboratory use, only those that are derived from WHO-approved sources and have a detailed history are acceptable for manufacture of human pharmaceuticals. A second new variable is the use of a genetically modified virus seed strain. Because the traditional vaccine strains are made by natural reassortment, they have escaped being labeled "genetically modified." This difference, although largely semantic, may affect the acceptance of the new vaccines. Before many of these traits can be tested, the virus must be amplified, inactivated, purified, and formulated for vaccine use.

In preparing for a pandemic threat, collaboration between government, industry, and academia is needed to overcome the obstacles and guarantee the most rapid production of a vaccine candidate. The recent SARS episode has shown that international collaboration in the face of a truly global threat is indeed possible.

The Safety Testing of Candidate Pandemic Vaccines

Unfortunately, there are only a few facilities available to carry out safety testing under the high-level biocontainment conditions required for handling highly pathogenic influenza viruses. Overcoming the technical hurdles to efficient vaccine production is only the start of a long, expensive process. Manufacturing scale-up presents its own problems, not least because plant workers will have no immunity to the pathogens they will be handling. Of prime importance is vaccine safety testing, but the need for safety testing will have to be balanced against the need for rapid mass production of a vaccine. In response to the 2003 H5N1 scare in Hong Kong, WHO has created an Interim Biosafety Risk Assessment guideline for the safety testing of pandemic vaccines, particularly the H5 and H7 subtypes, signifying a substantial advance in preparedness for the production of a pandemic influenza vaccine.

A major risk for all vaccine manufacturers is the occurrence of adverse reactions in a percentage of recipients. These reactions may be attributable to the vaccine, to the host, or (most likely) to a unique combination of the vaccine and the host genetic factors. Guillain-Barré syndrome in human beings first became apparent during the U.S. swine influenza vaccination program. The inevitability of adverse reactions underscores the product liability dilemma inherent in any vaccine program. The risk of devastating financial liability, and the unavailability or high cost of liability insurance, are increasingly discouraging vaccine manufacture, especially for universal use.

Legislative measures can be taken to reduce the impact of liability exposure. For example, the U.S. Congress passed the National Childhood Injury Compensation Act of 1986 (the "Vaccine Act"), which created a no-fault compensation program funded by an excise tax on vaccines. Plaintiffs need only establish that their injuries were caused by the vaccine. Claimants who are not satisfied with the administrative decision may still elect to sue the manufacturer, but the legal arguments available to the claimant are limited. Although the Vaccine Act represents progress in achieving a balance between consumer and manufacturer concerns, it would not apply to vaccines given to the general population, such as those for influenza or smallpox. Congress again attempted to address these concerns in a provision of the Homeland Security Act of 2002, and an Institute of Medicine panel is currently wrestling with the problem as well; however, drug manufacturers remain hesitant. The bottom line is that unless the government authorities of every country implement mechanisms that equitably limit vaccine liability, no prospective vaccine for H5N1, H7N7, or any other threatening influenza virus is likely to be produced for universal human use. It is hoped that governments will rise to the occasion after a crisis emerges, but logic suggests that the issue should be addressed now.

Antiviral Drugs

A global influenza strategy would call for the stockpiling of influenza antiviral drugs for use in the event of a pandemic until vaccines can be prepared. . . . The potential value of antivirals was demonstrated in the recent H7N7 outbreak in poultry and humans. Further, because epidemiological modeling has suggested that it is more infectious than SARS, influenza is unlikely to be controllable by SARS-like quarantine measures. The estimated 10 billion U.S. dollar cost of SARS and the societal disruption it caused in China and Toronto make a compelling case for stockpiling of antiviral drugs.

Pandemic influenza has already threatened twice in 2003. The events associated with these outbreaks show that we are in a much better position to rapidly respond to an influenza threat than we were in 1997; however, much remains to be accomplished. Overall, our state of preparedness is far from optimal.

Priorities to Ensure Pandemic Preparedness

To conclude, let us revisit the concern that the next influenza pandemic alert may involve a virus that has acquired the capacity to spread from human to human. What are the most urgent needs?

1) A sufficiently large supply of anti-influenza drugs to reduce the severity and spread of infection. Specific efficacious drugs are available, but no country has yet invested in stockpiling.

2) A vaccine matching the subtype of the emerging pandemic influenza strain that has been tested in clinical trials and for which manufacturers are prepared to "scale up" production. Such a vaccine would probably not match the emerging strain antigenically and would not prevent infection, but it could reduce the severity of illness until a matching vaccine is produced. Such vaccines have been discussed for 20 years. None is available, but specific plans to produce such a vaccine are currently being formulated.

3) The preparation, testing (safety and clinical trials), and availability of a vaccine derived by reverse genetics. The scientific technology is in place to achieve this goal, but manufacturing, intellectual property, and liability issues remain unresolved. In the event of a pandemic, reverse genetics would be the most rapid means by which to produce an antigenically matched vaccine. To be truly prepared, such a vaccine needs to be produced and tested now to identify and resolve the issues, rather than doing so in direct response to an emergency.

4) An improvement in the global influenza vaccine manufacturing capacity. . . . The country best prepared to meet this need is Canada; in Ontario, influenza vaccination is recommended and available at no charge to people of all ages during the influenza season. This progressive strategy during interpandemic years will

ensure the vaccine-manufacturing capacity of that region.

The conclusion of this analysis is inescapable: The world will be in deep trouble if the impending influenza pandemic strikes this week, this month, or even this year. It is now time to progress from talking about pandemic vaccines to taking action. Our hope is that the "Ontario experiment" will inspire other regions of the world to similarly promote the expansion of manufacturing capacity for influenza vaccines.

Although reverse genetics offers great advantages for the rapid preparation of influenza vaccine strains and for understanding pathogenesis, the reverse side of this benefit is its potential for the development of bioterrorism agents. Regardless of human endeavors, nature's ongoing experiments with H5N1 influenza in Asia and H7N7 in Europe may be the greatest bioterror threat of all. The time for talking is truly over. We must be prepared.

The Problem of Drug-Resistant Bacteria

By Peter Radetsky

Peter Radetsky is a contributing editor of *Discover* magazine and teaches in the Science Communication Program at the University of California at Santa Cruz. He has published articles and books on a variety of scientific topics, from multiple chemical sensitivity (MCS) to sports medicine to viruses. In the following article about the rise of drug-resistant bacteria, he summarizes the reasons for the evolution of so many drug-resistant bugs. Even though scientists have been aware that bacteria can develop drug resistance since the discovery of the first antibiotic, physicians and pharmaceutical companies did not believe resistance was a major problem with most drugs. Therefore, not only have antibiotics been overprescribed by physicians, but also they have been misused by patients and industries such as agriculture and the manufacturers of antibacterial products that currently flood the market. As humans battle bacteria, the bacteria fight back. They adapt ways to survive antibiotics, and then they share that adaptation with other bacteria. This ability will not disappear, so in Radetsky's opinion, scientists, manufacturers, physicians, and everyone who uses antibiotics will have to stop abusing them. At the same time, antibiotic development must continue, and researchers need to identify novel approaches for coexisting with bacteria. If not, Radetsky argues that people in industrialized countries will soon be reminded just how deadly bacterial infections can be.

Wells Shoemaker is a pediatrician in a small California town. Not too long ago he saw a patient new to the area, a little boy with a runny nose. "It's the same story every time," his

Peter Radetsky, "Last Days of the Wonder Drugs," *Discover*, vol. 19, 1998. Copyright © 1998 by The Walt Disney Company. Reproduced by permission of the author.

mother complained. "He starts out with a cold, and then his nose starts running green stuff, and then he gets an ear infection. He's only two years old, and he's already had four ear infections."

Shoemaker examined the child. He had a cold, all right, but his nasal fluid was clear, and he had no fever or bulging eardrums. No hint of an ear infection or any other bacterial attack. As Shoemaker offered his diagnosis, the mother interrupted: "The only thing that keeps him from getting an ear infection is antibiotics. My previous doctor used to give him antibiotics at the beginning of a cold. They worked great!"

"Antibiotics fight bacteria," Shoemaker explained. "Your son's cold is caused by a virus. He doesn't have an ear infection. But let's keep close tabs, and if he does begin to develop an infection, then we can turn to an antibiotic."

"But sometimes the doctor just prescribed them over the phone."

"Well, an antibiotic might prevent an infection, but it might not. It could even make way for a more aggressive germ that might cause an ear infection from hell. Then we'd have to resort to very, very powerful drugs with unpleasant side effects that have to be given by injection."

By this time the mother had heard enough. "I don't care! I know my child better than you do. I want antibiotics now!"

"I can't give them to you," Shoemaker replied. "In all good conscience, I just can't."

"Then I'm going to find another doctor, a doctor who cares about children!"

Stuart Levy would have been proud of the beleaguered pediatrician. Levy, a Tufts University School of Medicine microbiologist, is one of the world's loudest voices decrying the misuse of antibiotics. He writes books and articles about the problem, researches it in the lab, organizes conferences about it, presents it on TV. He's the founder of a worldwide network called the Alliance for the Prudent Use of Antibiotics. "We're in the midst of a crisis," he says, his baritone rising an octave. "We have to change things!"

Overprescription and Unneeded Drugs

The mother's conduct at the clinic was typical of what Levy laments: a patient demanding antibiotics for an illness that doesn't require them. What was not typical was that Shoemaker refused to give in. Many doctors do. And, like the child's previous pediatrician, many prescribe without ever being asked—even if antibiotics are not a suitable treatment. "At least half the human use of antibiotics in the United States is unnecessary or inappropriate," Levy says. "Either antibiotics are not indicated at all, or the wrong antibiotic is prescribed, or it's the wrong dosage or the wrong duration."

That leads to a lot of unneeded drugs. More than 50 million pounds of antibiotics are produced in the United States every year. Some 40 percent of that total is given to animals, mostly to promote growth rather than treat disease. Antibiotic use is also rampant in agriculture—for example, the drugs are sprayed onto fruit trees to control bacterial infections. Another little-recognized application is in antibacterial household cleaning products, soaps, toothpaste, and even plastic toys and cutting boards, which incorporate bacteria-killing substances too potent to be used in the body. The upshot of this massive exposure is the increasingly familiar predicament the world now faces: disease-causing bugs that resist the drugs that once thwarted them. We are experiencing an alarming resurgence of common but no longer curable infections from bugs that developed their resistance in our antibiotic-filled bodies, in animals, in fields, even on our antibacterial-soaked kitchen counters. It's what Levy calls "the antibiotic paradox." The miracle drugs themselves are destroying the miracle. And it may be too late to do much about it.

The magnitude of the problem is startling. At least two dozen different kinds of bacteria have developed resistance to one or more antibiotics. Some strains of three life-threatening species—the blood poisoners Enterococcus faecalis and Pseudomonas aeruginosa, and Mycobacterium tuberculosis, the TB bug—now frustrate every single antibiotic known, more than 100 different drugs. Ubiquitous pathogens such as *Streptococcus, Staphylococcus*, and *Pneumococcus*, which among them cause ear, nose, and throat infections, scarlet fever, meningitis, and pneumonia, are becoming widely resistant. The possibility that these common childhood diseases might become completely unresponsive to treatment is a physician's—and a parent's—nightmare.

Hospital records suggest the scope of the problem. While there are no figures on how many people enter hospitals already infected, over 2 million fall prey to microbes once they get there, in this country alone. Some 90,000 die. About 70 percent of those are infected by drug-resistant bacteria. Costs for treatment of these infections approach $5 billion a year. Overall, the yearly toll exacted by drug-resistant infections in the United States is estimated to exceed $30 billion. "The multiresistant organisms of the 1990s are a grim warning of the possibility of the post-antibiotic era," states the Centers for Disease Control and Prevention (CDC) in Atlanta.

But why? The answer involves equal parts complacency, economics, and simply the nature of nature. It's been known that bacteria can become resistant to antibiotics almost since the first one, penicillin, was discovered seven decades ago. . . .

"Geneticists certainly talked about the problem, but nobody was going to do anything about it until it slapped you in the face," recalls Rockefeller University molecular geneticist Joshua Lederberg, who has consulted for the pharmaceutical industry since the 1950s. "There were enough instances of the occurrence of resistance in this, that, and the other place, but it didn't seem that urgent."

In the mid-1970s, two dangerous bugs almost simultaneously became resistant to penicillin: *Haemophilus influenzae*, which induces respiratory infections, and *Neisseria gonorrhoeae*, the cause of the venereal disease gonorrhea. In fact, not only did they become resistant but they developed the ability to flat out destroy the drug. And both bacteria displayed the very same resistance gene—most likely it had been transferred to them from bacteria living in the gastrointestinal tract. Gonorrhea resistance was initially discovered in the Philippines in servicemen suffering from venereal disease. From there, it was traced to prostitutes in Vietnam who had been given penicillin regularly as a precautionary measure. That overexposure engendered resistance. Today every country in the world is bedeviled by drug-resistant gonorrhea.

Here was a graphic example of the power of antibiotic resistance—and its ability to spread. And still the medical and pharmaceutical communities, which were accruing enormous profits from antibiotics, were not alarmed. Says Levy, "I remember talks about resistant *E. coli* and *Salmonella* at an American Society for Microbiology meeting in the early seventies. People said, 'Oh, isn't that interesting, but let me know when something serious comes along.'"

Slow and Costly Research and Development

"You have to understand that a lot of these decisions were made not by scientists but by marketing-type people," says David Shlaes, vice president of infectious-disease research at American Home Products' Wyeth-Ayerst research unit. "They were looking at a marketplace they thought was saturated—there were a gazillion antibiotics—and satisfied. They didn't hear many complaints from general practitioners about resistance. It was only the scientists who were worried. When you don't get complaints from people you're selling your products to, you may not listen very hard. And they didn't."

Dramatically escalating costs of developing new drugs and more stringent regulatory requirements imposed by the U.S. Food and Drug Administration further dampened the drug industry's appetite for jumping into new antibiotic research and development.

The result was virtual paralysis in antibiotic development just when the resistance was careening out of control. "In 1991 an informal survey among pharmaceutical companies in the United States and Japan suggested that at least 50 percent of them had either diminished substantially or totally gotten out of anti-bacterial research," says Shlaes. "People simply sloughed off the problem of resistance."

But it's no surprise that bugs should develop resistance to our efforts to wipe them out. It's only natural for an organism to do everything it can to evade its killer. By developing new drugs, we attempt to stay one step ahead of our microbial enemies, and the microbes furiously return the favor. Antibiotics actually promote resistance. For example, let's say that Shoemaker's young patient was indeed suffering from an ear infection. An antibiotic might wipe out most of those bad bugs, but a few might survive. If the child's besieged immune system were capable of mopping up, all would be well. But if it weren't, with the susceptible bacteria now dead, the resistant strains could spread like weeds through a newly harvested field. And if the child didn't take the entire prescribed course of drugs, or if they were the wrong kind, more resistant strains might propagate.

To compound the problem, antibiotics don't just kill bad bugs—like a huge scythe, they also cut down innocent bystanders. That's unfortunate, says Levy. "Non-disease-causing bacteria are essential parts of the body's natural armor against invading infectious bacteria." These benign microbes limit the spread of their dangerous brethren simply by being in the way. With them gone, the field is even more wide open for resistant bugs to proliferate. . . .

Resistance Strategies

The range of microbial resistance strategies is mind-boggling. Mutation is one approach. . . . But by itself mutation might not be enough to generate widespread resistance. The microbes' ace in the hole is their ability to share resistance genes. One way they do so is by means of a kind of bacterial sex in which a bug carrying a resistance gene meets a susceptible mate, snags it with a narrow tube, reels the bug in, then transfers its gene. Bacteria aren't picky about who receives their gift. It might be another bug of the same species, it might not.

Another method involves simply vacuuming up scraps of loose DNA that have been released by dead cells in the vicinity. If the housekeeping microbe is lucky, a resistance gene may be lurking in one of these DNA snippets. And sometimes bacteria receive help in swapping genes. Viruses called bacteriophages can infect a bug and by chance whisk away its resistance gene and deposit it in another microbe.

If the methods of swapping genes are ingenious, so are the resistance mechanisms they engender. Some bacterial genes produce pumps that transport antibiotics out of the organism before they have a chance to do any harm. Others generate powerful enzymes that inactivate the drugs. Others modify the antibiotics' targets within the microbes or provide decoys that divert and disable the drugs.

Bacteria have used such survival strategies for millions of years, but now things are different. A few drops of "mold juice" have exploded into millions of pounds of bug-killing drugs. Never before have bacteria encountered such colossal evolutionary pressure. Humans are pushing microbial evolution into overdrive. It's a supercharged arms race. . . .

The result: Superbugs that can withstand not just one but multitudes of antibiotics. Superbugs that display resistance to the newest antibiotics even before they are formally introduced. Diseases that no longer respond to our attempts to prevent or cure them. It's a new age, all right, but no longer golden.

Eleventh-Hour Scramble

Is it too late to do anything? Are we spiraling back to a pre-antibiotic world in which we are reduced to trying to avoid infection and, failing that, helplessly hoping for the best?

Not if pharmaceutical companies have anything to say about it. Finally, belatedly, the industry is scrambling to avert such a catastrophe.

"The turnaround occurred in the mid-nineties," says Shlaes. "The major event was the epidemic of resistant *Enterococcus*— that really made an impact on people. And there was the continuing spread of multiresistant staph around the world.

"In the next five to ten years we're going to see new and novel kinds of antibiotics coming out of drug companies," Shlaes predicts. "I'm optimistic. But it's not going to be soon."

So even if these new drugs prove to be effective—and there's no assurance of that—what are we going to do in the meantime? Stuart Levy suggests an approach he calls prudent use. His hope is that if we can get antibiotic use under control, with physicians prescribing appropriately, according to more precise diagnoses; if animal and agricultural use is pared down to the bare essentials; and if household disinfectants are no longer spiked with lingering bug killers, then we might be able to turn back the clock. The good bugs might supplant the bad, and our existing drugs might once more be able to shoulder the load.

Levy's hope rests on a basic tenet of evolution: if you get something, you generally have to give up something. In acquiring antibiotic-fighting capabilities, it seems, bacteria have to divert energy from other needs. Some resistant bugs just don't reproduce well, for example—they have a tough time making the necessary protein building blocks for their offspring. It's evolution's quid pro quo. If this enormous pressure on bugs to develop resistance were curbed, the hope is, the remaining susceptible microbes might outstrip their more muscular, but relatively barren, brethren. And back we'd go to the golden age.

Don't count on it, advises population and evolutionary biologist Bruce Levin. He points to a T-shirt hanging in his office at Emory University in Atlanta. Printed on the back is the statement You Can't Go Back Again. Recent experiments have led him to that bleak assessment.

Two years ago Levin and his student Bassam Tomeh sampled bacteria from the diapers of 25 toddlers at a nearby day-care center. When they isolated samples of the common gut bacteria *Escherichia coli*, they found that a quarter were resistant to the antibiotic streptomycin. At first glance the find is disturbing but not remarkable—after all, drug-resistant *E. coli* has become an ominous fact of today's life. But a closer look raises red flags. "Doctors have almost never used streptomycin in the last 30 years," Levin exclaims. For some reason, these bacteria are holding on to hard-to-maintain defenses that are no longer needed. . . .

"Maybe Bruce is right," concedes Levy. "Maybe you can't go back again in terms of converting resistant bacteria back to susceptible ones. But that's not the point. The point is that it's a numbers game." The numbers he's talking about involve the ratio between resistant and susceptible bacteria. If resistant bugs predominate, then yes, their inability to revert to susceptibility is important. But if susceptibles outnumber resistants, then the more vulnerable bugs may carry the day despite the intransigence of the others. Levy is fond of citing a French study showing that when people whose guts were plagued by resistant E. coli ate only sterilized food, the nature of the prevailing microbes changed. Susceptible bugs once more outnumbered resistants. Either the resistant bacteria had been strengthened by reinforcements entering with commercial foods, or the food contained antibiotics that induced the microbes to propagate while destroying their competition. Bugless, drugless, sterilized food reversed the trend.

Trying to Thwart Resistant Bugs

Three U.S. hospital-based studies showing that resistant bugs disappear with the withdrawal of antibiotics drive home the point. At the Veterans Affairs Medical Center in Minneapolis, when the antibiotic gentamicin was no longer given for infections by a variety of resistant gut bacteria, including *E. coli*, the levels of resistance dropped accordingly. Studies at the Veterans Affairs Medical Centers in Tucson [Arizona] and Richmond, Virginia, chronicle similar results with the antibiotic clindamycin and resistant diarrhea-causing bacteria called *Clostridium difficile*. Get rid of clindamycin and you get rid of resistant bugs—within months.

"That's pretty dramatic data," Levy says. "It tells us that there's a flux of bacteria coming and going. Some stay and some go. We want the susceptibles to stay."

One way to accomplish that may be to seed our bodies with benign, drug-susceptible bugs. It's an approach that Madrid-based microbiologist Fernando Baquero calls ecological intervention. "This should be envisaged as an ecological problem—ecology for our gut," he explains. "Resistant bugs are modifying our normal flora. Our flora has evolved with us from the beginning of the human species. We don't know about the long-term consequences of the alteration of this normal ecology. What we should have are reserves of susceptible bacteria to recolonize us. We should make susceptible-bacteria banks."

Levy agrees. "Let's just bring in the susceptibles and get rid of the resistants. For example, bring in susceptible E. coli. Drink it, day in and day out. What do you think is going to happen? Resistant strains are going to stay there? No! They're going to be shed and the susceptibles take over."

This very approach is being used in animal husbandry. In March [1998] the FDA approved a spray containing 29 types of bacteria isolated from the guts of mature chickens. These are the bugs that chicks would normally receive from their mothers but that hatchery-born chicks lack. Once sprayed with the mix, the chicks ingest the bacteria while preening themselves.

So far the results have been promising (and in Japan, where the spray has been available for more than a year, it has been highly successful). Not only does the spray of good bugs protect the chicks from pathogenic bacteria—in particular Salmonella—simply by occupying the niches where the bad bugs would otherwise lodge, but it discourages antibiotic use. Because why would anyone want to give these animals antibiotics that would kill off the very bugs that are protecting them?

Education and Restraint

Levy considers this approach a model of what can be done in humans. But the list of changes that must accompany such an approach is daunting: education and more accurate diagnoses leading to fewer, and more appropriate, prescriptions of antibiotics; restrained use of antibiotics in animal husbandry and agriculture; reduced use of antibacterials in household disinfectants. And all this not only in the United States but in countries worldwide, some of which are even more profligate with antibiotics.

"There's a lot of ingrained social behavior associated with antibiotic use," observes Levin. To wit, Shoemaker's unhappy encounter and Levin's own experience at the day-care center. "The majority of the kids were on antibiotics during the six months we did the study. At least one kid was on five different antibiotics. Another was on triple antibiotic therapy—prophylactically! She wasn't even sick." He shrugs his shoulders. "And the parents of these kids were from Emory and the CDC. So it wasn't exactly an unenlightened group. How are you going to change most people's minds if you can't change theirs?"

And what if, after all is said and done, prudent use can be implemented—what if it just doesn't make a difference? The years to come may be grim, indeed, seared by a hard reality the more fortunate parts of the world have not had to face for the last half-century. The bugs are reminding us who's boss.

The Threat of Germ Warfare

By Tara O'Toole and Thomas V. Inglesby

Doctors Tara O'Toole and Thomas V. Inglesby are director and deputy director of the Center for Biosecurity at the University of Pittsburgh Medical Center. They are also coeditors-in-chief for the new magazine *Biosecurity and Bioterrorism: Biodefense Strategy, Practice, and Science.* In their opening editorial, excerpted in the following selection, O'Toole and Inglesby summarize the threat of bioweapons and the need for organized, global research and preparation. There is a real possibility that mass destruction might not come from a large mushroom cloud or huge chemical release, the authors say, but from a germ whose secret release would not be noticeable until the resulting epidemic was well under way. The production of bioweapons does not require huge resources or large industry; the knowledge and materials are available to most anyone. This fact makes bioweapons attractive to those who could not possibly battle a much larger, richer enemy with conventional attacks. To counter this growing threat, O'Toole and Inglesby state that the United States needs to mobilize the government, professional communities, and industries in a cooperative effort to spur biodefense research and to expand the medical and public health capabilities for handling epidemics.

O ne of the most important characteristics of our era is the prospect that powerful destructive technologies will be wielded by terrorist groups who wish to kill as many people as possible. While such prospects are becoming increasingly likely, they are not inevitable. To prevent such catastrophes, we must be able to imagine the tragic possibilities before us with the vividness and analytical precision necessary to establish co-

Tara O'Toole and Thomas V. Inglesby, "Toward Biosecurity," *Biosecurity and Bioterrorism: Biodefense Strategy, Practice, and Science*, vol. 1, February 6, 2003. Copyright © 2003 by Mary Ann Liebert, Inc. Reproduced by permission.

herent priorities and a course of action. We must begin with acknowledgement of some deeply disturbing realities.

Of the various plausible forms of terrorist attack against civilian populations, only attacks with nuclear or biological weapons have the capacity to cause mass casualties—potentially tens of thousands of deaths—in a single blow. Nuclear weapons are widely recognized as strategic threats to nations and civilizations, but the strategic danger posed by biological weapons is not as widely understood. Moreover, the actions needed to reduce the threat of biological weapons have only recently received concerted attention. Although chemical weapons can cause great suffering and terror and require specific preparation and response protocols, they are not capable of inflicting massive lethality and do not pose strategic threats to national survival. The convention of lumping nuclear, chemical, radiological ("dirty bomb"), and biological weapons together as "weapons of mass destruction" is misleading and hinders prevention of and preparation for these different threats.

The Production of Bioweapons

Biological weapons can be manufactured with materials and knowhow that are openly available, dispersed around the planet, and hard to track. There are no theoretical limits to the amounts of bioweapons agents that can be manufactured or the number of targets that could be attacked. Best estimates are that about a dozen states now have active bioweapons programs, though it is exceedingly difficult to detect bioweapons production efforts or to distinguish legitimate biotechnological enterprises from weapons production. Some effort has been made to secure the enormous bioweapons enterprise operated by the former Soviet Union, but thousands of former bioweapons scientists remain unemployed, and Russia has yet to allow independent inspectors into some facilities that functioned as bioweapons plants during the Cold War.

Bioweapons will become increasingly diverse and potent as a result of discoveries being made in the life sciences—discoveries that are essential to progress in medicine, agriculture, and environmental stewardship. Governments will be greatly tempted to declare some segments of bioscience "off limits" or to sequester certain kinds of knowledge behind a shroud of secrecy. Such tactics in the quest for biosecurity are likely to bring only partial and temporary respite—at best—and could wreak tremendous damage upon science, the world economy, and public trust.

Bioweapons can be made without the technological resources of an industrialized state. Such weapons may be particularly attractive to terrorists seeking to inflict devastating harm on nations whose military might makes conventional attacks impractical. As has been shown by the search for those who mailed *B. anthracis*-laden letters to government officials and media outlets in 2001, it is (and will remain) difficult to assign attribution for covert bioattacks. If a bioattack leaves no return address or it is committed by a terrorist group without a country to defend, traditional deterrence strategies—"If you hurt us, we will destroy what you most value"—will be ineffective.

Finally, covert delivery of a biological or nuclear weapon is far more likely than an attack using missiles. Catastrophic terrorist attacks do not require high-performance, superpower-quality weapons delivery systems. Simply transporting a nuclear weapon or a bioweapon to the place where it is to be detonated or dispersed can assure mass casualties.

The Response to Bioweapons

The collective human reaction to the danger presented by bioterrorism and bioweapons proliferation has thus far been strangely subdued. In the U.S., the federal government has begun to address the national capacity to cope with the deliberate epidemics that would follow bioweapons attacks. Incremental progress has occurred in some areas. For example, state health departments received federal funds in fiscal year (FY) 2002 to improve bioterrorism preparedness; in FY 2003, the National Institutes of Health (NIH) will receive $1.7 billion for biodefense-related research and development, a significant increase from the $151 million appropriated for this purpose in FY 2002; production of a U.S. smallpox vaccine stockpile is underway, and plans for vaccinating against smallpox are being formulated at federal and local levels. Thus far, the individual initiatives begun to improve bioterrorism preparedness do not add up to a coherent strategy, on either the national or international level, for dealing with the problem of bioweapons, nor do the actions underway accurately reflect the urgency or magnitude of the perils that confront us.

Much can be done to prevent the development and use of bioweapons and to lessen the suffering, death, and disruption that could result from bioterrorist attacks. Governments alone cannot meet the challenges posed by bioterrorism, however. To achieve biosecurity—a security that is grounded in liberty, intellectual freedom, and respect for human life—it will be necessary to enlist the genius of innovative individuals and to engage institutions, professional communities, and industries. The problems posed by mass lethality bioweapons are global; ultimately, the solutions must be as well.

Biodefense Research and Development

Substantial scientific and technological progress will remain fundamental to improving national and international biodefense capacity. In the near term, we should seek to create effective diagnostic tests, medicine, and vaccines to counter attacks involving the most likely bioagents. In the longer term, we should use our technical prowess to shift the advantage from the offense to the defense, so that even attacks using sophisticated, bioengineered weapons will fail to cause large numbers of fatalities. Such a response capacity will compel us to delve deeply into the science of human immune function, the mechanisms of pathogenesis, and other aspects of the science of infectious disease, and it will require that we establish the capacity to rapidly produce and distribute large quantities of appropriate vaccines and medicines.

Improved Medical and Public Health Capacities

A robust biodefense strategy will require significant preparation and organizational innovation within health care institutions and the public health community. Not within living memory has America been called upon to cope with mass casualty disasters, nor have we had to manage large-scale, fast-moving epidemics. The infrastructures now available to handle these threats are insufficient to the task. Preparing for bioterrorism, without harming the peacetime missions of medicine and public health—missions that are themselves crucial to a healthy society—will require substantial and sustained investments of talent and money.

The most desirable and most effective solution to the bioterrorism problem is prevention. We must, over time, develop the intelligence capacities and technologies needed to detect bioweapons development and to interdict bioterrorist attacks before they take place. We will need to devise legal frameworks that provide assurance that nations and groups are not establishing bioweapons arsenals or pursuing bioterrorism. But treaties, laws, and regulations will not be sufficient to prevent bioterrorism. There is an intimate and indissoluble linkage between legitimate, critically important bioscientific research and potential malignant applications of such knowledge. It will not be possible to prevent bioweapons development and use without the active and willing participation of the scientific community. . . .

We Must Act

The dangers and challenges posed by the bioterrorist threat are daunting—and the threat is growing. The United States and the collective international community can eliminate bioweapons as agents of mass lethality. To accomplish this, the nature of the threat must be understood in greater detail by a wide range of leaders and by the public. We must take the steps needed to improve the ability of key institutions to respond effectively to deliberate epidemics. We must muster the technical expertise and scientific and managerial talent needed to create an arsenal of drugs and vaccines essential to saving the lives of victims of bioterrorist attacks. We must create a coherent system of social contracts, including professional standards and legal strictures, so that legitimate bioscience research can proceed without fueling a bioweapons arms race. Many are already laboring mightily, in both government and civilian sectors, to diminish and blunt the possible dangers of bioweapons. . . . Together, we must muster the will and the wisdom to ensure the responsible use of biological knowledge and the technologies it makes possible.

Understanding the Relationship Between People and Germs

By Joshua Lederberg

Dr. Joshua Lederberg is an American geneticist and microbiologist who received the Nobel Prize in 1958 for his work in bacterial genetics. Though he has been involved in research in artificial intelligence and NASA programs, as well as consulted on health issues for the government and the World Health Organization, his life's work has been in microbial genetics. He has been a vocal proponent of dropping the metaphor of a war on germs in exchange for understanding the coexistence of germs and humans. Microbes are part of the global ecology and part of the individual ecology of every human. Lederberg states that not enough is known about the natural balance of humans and the microbes that live within them. No species exists in isolation from another; and so, no species should be studied and, in the case of infectious microbes, destroyed or controlled without knowledge of its consequences to humanity or the environment. The author argues that past efforts at controlling disease-causing bacteria and viruses have left people vulnerable to many of the bugs that were thought to be under control. Therefore, according to Lederberg, the challenge today is to understand the details of the host-parasite relationship so that more directed, more successful therapies can be aimed at controlling dangerous germs.

Joshua Lederberg, "Getting in Tune with the Enemy—Microbes," *The Scientist*, vol. 17, June 2, 2003, p. 20. Copyright © 2003 by *The Scientist*. Reproduced by permission of Copyright Clearance Center, Inc.

After a lapse of some decades, germs and disease have again been very much on our minds, largely because of the dreadful effect of AIDS throughout the world. We also have had a reawakened consciousness that globally prevalent diseases like tuberculosis and malaria remain historical scourges. Now [in 2003] the daily news tells us of new outbreaks such as severe acute pulmonary syndrome, or SARS, spreading from China, with an outcome that cannot be confidently predicted at this time.

Throughout history, infectious disease has regulated lives. Only in the 20th century, thanks to simple hygienic measures like washing our hands regularly and separating drinking water from sewage runoff, have we taken a larger role in trying to control how microbes affect human life.

A child born in the United States in 1900 had an average life expectancy of 47 years. By the end of that century, mainly because of our conquest of infectious disease, it was 80 years for women and 75 or so for men. Since the late 1920s, the metaphor we optimistically adopted concerning our relationship to germs has been that of the "microbe hunters'" conquest over specific diseases. By the 1960s, reinforced by the wonder drugs and vaccines of mid-century, many were claiming that "plagues will be forever banished from Earth" only to be humbled after the tragic advent of the AIDS epidemic. SARS is today's new challenge.

Rather than being satisfied with the metaphor of conquest and the notion of eradication of infectious disease, we should learn a more nuanced lesson: that we had best aspire to a relationship of symbiotic (mutually beneficial) coexistence with germs. Multitudes of bacteria and viruses occupy our skin, our mucous membranes and our intestinal tracts, and we must learn to live with them in a "truce" rather than victory. Understanding this cohabitation of genomes within the human body—what I call the microbiome—is central to understanding the dynamics of health and disease.

Microbes Evolve Quickly and Easily

From an evolutionary point of view, microbes are extremely successful. They can grow and evolve in cycles of 20 minutes or less. A community of a billion cells can be replaced overnight from a single seed. Tens of billions of cells can be cultured in a single small test tube.

By contrast, the human species has a total population of less than 10 billion, quite modest on the microbial scale. Each human is multicellular and large, with a costly, long developmental cycle. Unlike people, germs readily exchange genes within and between various species. They don't speciate or differentiate into genetically isolated organisms as we do. In fact, these bugs engage in promiscuous lateral gene transfer, making the microbial world a kind of [gene-]based worldwide Web that shares genetic information that can move from one bug to another.

When, for example, antibiotics get into our sewage system and kill some bugs, it is the occasional resistant mutant that survives. These survivors can then transfer their newfound immunity to the genes of other microbes, including pathogenic species that foment human disease.

These rapidly evolving bugs can gang up on humans through synergies of organisms that provoke mild disease, which, when joined with others, become virulent. This may prove to be the case with SARS, which appears to be a variation of the common cold virus. Humans, by contrast, are not only genetically isolated from other species (we get no biological benefit from evolutionary innovations in mice or monkeys), but the cells of the human germ line are sealed off in our gonads, insulated from most of the vicissitudes (changes) of the body. Whatever that body might learn by way of generating immunity, let's say against a new virus, cannot be passed on to one sperm or egg to the next generation. New generations have to learn it all over again.

Pathogens Need Live Hosts

In short, the competitive evolutionary odds seem cast very much in favor of the bugs. We see this mismatch when great plagues and epidemics sweep the world. By the raw evidence, the capability of evolving bugs should have trounced us eons ago.

So why haven't they? Why are we still here, sharing the planet with the bugs? They haven't extinguished us simply because microbes have a shared interest in the survival of the host, humans and other multicellular creatures. The bug that kills its host is at a dead end.

Biologically speaking, the reason we are still here is because microbes need live hosts for their own survival. This reality allows us to establish some of the ground rules of evolutionary success in the microbial world. It is as if they have read the Bible and know Genesis: They go forth and disseminate as their first rule. They multiply. Next, according to Malthusian and Darwinian doctrine, they have to be the fittest in order to survive so that they can produce the largest number of offspring they can.

Then they face a dilemma: If they extinguish their host too quickly, they will not be able to propagate. But, of course, they also have an imperative of securing a lodging post in the host, a bridgehead, fighting off local defenses and establishing a reservoir for dissemination. This is what disease as experienced by humans is all about: the establishment of a foothold so the obliging host will provide warm food and shelter and be domesticated to the service of that parasite. In fact, the symptoms of disease that we see are very often exploited on behalf of the bug's capacity to disseminate.

For example, once an organism like cholera gets into your gut, it provokes intense diarrhea. To create diarrhea, cholera secretes a hormone that results in the release of water in the gut. As long as the patient plays the game of massive rehydration, he is likely to balance the loss of fluid, survive and also have disseminated the bugs by the billions.

Cholera doesn't "want" to hurt us, but its survival as a species depends on polluting water supplies. The disease is then transmitted to other hosts. If it could get away with never killing its host, it would be even better off.

Symbiotic Coexistence with Microbes

Sometimes a germ will even protect the host against other competing pathogens. And the best strategy of all is to fuse with the host by becoming part of the host's genome.

Today, we are carrying around 500 different integrated retroviruses [viruses with ribonucleic acid (RNA) for their genetic material] in our own genome [genetic material]. After millions of years of evolution, the ancient viruses now perform indispensable defense functions for the host. The microbes that co-inhabit our bodies show considerable self-restraint by moderating the virulence of disease, especially in well-established relationships with animal hosts. Systemic pathogens (that can affect the entire body) such as staphylococci and streptococci, that long ago invaded us and now live within our bodies, rarely secrete extreme toxins. In consequence, probably a third of us are walking around as healthy carriers of these bugs.

It would thus broaden our philosophical horizons if we thought of a human as more than an organism. We are superorganisms with an extended genome that includes not only our own cells but also the fluctuating microbial genome set of bacteria and viruses that share our bodies. Some of these onetime invaders have become permanently established in our cells, even crossed the boundary line and entered our own genome. I call that extended set of companions the microbiome, and I pray for more research on how they affect our lives, besides the flare-ups, the blunders we call disease.

We need more research, not only on how bacteria are virulent but how they withhold their virulence and moderate their attacks. We need to investigate how our microbiome flora, the ones we live with all the time, don't cause disease and instead protect us against their competitors. We need to find a cooperative arrangement, a truce with those microbes that don't kill us.

CHAPTER 4

Germ
Controversies

Antimicrobial Products Are Mostly Unnecessary

By Hanna Rosin

Journalist Hanna Rosin is a *Washington Post* reporter who also contributes to the *New Republic*. In 1997 she did a detailed article about America's obsession with germs, from which the following is excerpted. Rosin presents America's past and present episodes of germophobia, which she implies has currently reached ridiculous proportions. Fueled by microbiologists who sample everyday surfaces and publish scary names of microbes and numbers beyond comprehension (ten-to-the-fifth colony forming units [CFUs]), many Americans are deceived into thinking their own homes are dangerously contaminated, Rosin argues. This fear, which cannot be justified by actual risk assessments, has led to the explosion of antimicrobial products that flood the market today. Whether the risk is real or perceived, manufacturers are more than happy to capitalize on it. But Rosin contends that the average adult does not need this myriad of antimicrobial products nor a hyperclean lifestyle to live a healthy life.

O n April 6 [1997], *PrimeTime Live* aired one of its periodic warnings to consumers. "Now a story about hidden dangers right in your own kitchen," Diane Sawyer intoned—then introduced Karen Peters, a trim, chipper young housewife. Peters was supposed to be the American everywoman, perhaps even a little better than that. She was the above average neat type, cleaning and wiping often during dinner, the narrator explained. "I'm compulsive," shrugged Peters, "What can I say?" Her husband agreed. "I like things very neat. That's why I married her," he joked.

The Peters household was chosen as one of ten to participate in a *PrimeTime* experiment. The *PrimeTime* team swabbed Mrs. Peters's drains, cutting boards, counters, refrigerator handles, sponges, and dishrags—then sent the samples to a lab for analysis. The results were alarming: scores of food-borne bacteria—*salmonella, campylobacter, staphylococcus, listeria,* and *E. coli*—lurked on all the kitchen surfaces. The highest count of E. coli came from Mrs. Peters's kitchen. "Of all ten?" asked the crumpled Peters. "Oh my God." To compound her mortification, *PrimeTime* subjected Mrs. Peters to yet another experiment. They covered her kitchen with a harmless powder called germ glow that mimics the spread of bacteria, but is visible only under ultraviolet light. When they turned on the light, the house was a war zone, with a fake germ dust staining the cutting board, her hands, the sink, the faucet handle, and "most worrisome," her son Preston's face. "Oh my gosh. . . . Oh my God. Oh Preston."

The New Germophobia

Welcome to America's new zone of germ warfare: your own kitchen. It used to be that germs invaded our shores from distant and unclean lands, through rhesus monkeys brought over from Africa, strawberries from Mexico, raspberries from Guatemala. But now we can't escape, because the deadly critters are hiding under our own roofs. "We've discovered a whole new range of hot zones," says Dr. Charles Gerba, a microbiologist at the University of Arizona and a consultant on the *PrimeTime Live* episode. "And most of them are in our kitchens." Run away to protect yourself: "It's safer to eat out than home," warns Gerba. The rhesus monkey has come home to roost.

The truth is, of course, we haven't "discovered" anything: the germs have always been there, even in our kitchen sink. We have in fact so thoroughly conquered germs this century that we've raised our life expectancy by twenty years. Yet somehow Americans are convinced they are under massive internal attack. In a recent *CBS News* poll, 39 percent of Americans said they are "very" conscious of germs. One in five has a close friend or family member who is "obsessed" with germs. Thirty-nine percent said their concern about germs has caused them to change their kitchen cleaning habits, according to a poll by the company 3M. City dwellers are especially skittish. More than half polled by CBS said that, in order to avoid contact with germs, they don't touch subway handles, public telephones, or airplane headrests.

What explains this new germophobia? The AIDS epidemic probably has something to do with it, although the HIV virus has never been perceived as a mainstream middle-class killer. Also, it is widely known that you can't get AIDS from a doorknob. There are more reported incidents of food poisoning these days, but that's mostly because the Centers for Disease Control and state health departments only recently started counting, and newspapers have started writing about it: the number of stories about germs has increased twentyfold in the last four years, according to a count by [the company] Farberware. But really, there are no more germs—certainly not more than a few years ago. There's just more reporting of germs in more locations than ever before. The problem can only be explained with a paradox: as a society gets richer and cleaner, it searches for dirt in ever more remote places.

The Antibacterial Market

In this manic search, the market is only too happy to help. Over the last year, a new category of "antibacterial" product has emerged on the shelves. From 1992 to 1997, the number of new antibacterial products introduced has increased from 36 to 140, according to *Product Alert* magazine. And that only includes ordinary household goods, such as soaps, cutting boards, and kitchen cleaners. By now, almost all companies that make plastic cutting boards have stopped producing anything but the more expensive antibacterial kind. Antibacterial soaps and cleaners have captured 50 percent of their $2.1 billion market. More obscure products are showing up as well. Over the next year, Farberware will introduce a line of fifty new antibacterial gadgets, ranging from pizza cutters to nail brushes to cheese graters. Pens and candles are under consideration. More than half of Americans already say they go out of their way to buy antibacterial products whenever available, while 93 percent say they use at least one such product.

It is already possible to spend most of your day in germ-free comfort. You can get a good night's sleep on an antibacterial pillow, snuggled under an antibacterial blanket, brush your teeth with antibacterial toothpaste, take a shower with antibacterial soap, dry off with an antibacterial towel, pull on your antibacterial socks and underwear, eat breakfast on your antibacterial tray, say goodbye to Spot in his antibacterial dog bed, give little Suzie her antibacterial toy, grab a cookie from an antibacterial jar, spray the bus seat (and your office phone) with antibacterial cleaner, then come home, and chop up some celery with your antibacterial knife.

This is not the first, or even the second, time America has become obsessed with cleanliness. The history of American social and economic progress could be told as a tale of progressively cleaner kitchens. The first big push came after the Civil War, when armies of health reformers swept through city slums. They confused germs with filth, but never mind, they meant well. The point was to teach everyone the new standards of American middle-class cleanliness, so rich and poor alike could participate in the march of progress. [American educator and civil rights activist] Booker T. Washington preached the "gospel of the toothbrush" to former slaves. For women, the crusade meant rising "above the beaten paths of cookery and needleworth," as [American author and] reformer Harriette Plunkett put it. Later on, the discipline of home economics added a pseudo-scientific twist, as pamphlets from the '30s explained to the twentieth-century housewife that a "pin-point of dust" could yield "three thousand living organisms." (Back then there were hucksters too; [Texas gardener] William Radam became a millionaire in 1890 selling a drop of wine in hot water labeled "Microbe Killer Number One.") And soap companies urged Americans to coach new immigrants on "American ways of keeping house," as an ad for Fels-Naptha soap explained.

The apex came, of course, in the 1950's, when the middle-class fantasies of earlier ads became an American reality. Suddenly the country became the cleanest in the world, building the most bathrooms, using the most water. Like today, new household gadgets multiplied by the dozens, from Tide, promising the "cleanest clean," to the most revolutionary, the garbage disposal. Ads featured happy housewives beaming near their sparkling new blenders; all was well in the world.

Fear and Isolation

If the old movement for cleanliness made Americans feel hopeful about their future, the new push is likely to bring on terror and depression. The old one united the country in a national program of uplift; the new one isolates us in our squalid homes. Charles Gerba is one of a handful of researchers in America pioneering a new field called household microbiology, which studies the home as the source of most food-related illnesses. Gerba is a guy who sprays public benches with disinfectant before a picnic, and turns on public rest room faucets with his elbow. Spend a few hours with his research and you too will become suspicious of everything you touch. He passes his time swabbing gas station toilets, hotel pillows, office coffee cups, and his own washing machine. His research papers have titles like "A Microbial Survey of Office Coffee Cups" and "Enteric Contamination of Public Restrooms."

Gerba's work has the strange and disheartening effect of seeming to reverse years of progress. It is much safer, he says, to eat a sandwich in your bathroom than your kitchen, because years of scrubbing bathrooms with disinfectants have made the toilet the cleanest place in the house. Neglected kitchens, meanwhile, have become hotbeds for germs. Bachelors keep perhaps the cleanest houses, he says, because they never clean, while the rest of us wipe furiously with our microbe-soaked sponges and spread the germs everywhere. His latest laboratory is the laundry room, and based on initial results, things look pretty ugly. "It's a lot worse than I ever thought," he says about washing machines. "Fecal bacteria and hepatitis survive the average washing. Even salmonella survives to some extent, and spreads from one dirty item to the rest of the clothes." He suggests running the machine empty with just bleach and water between every load to kill the lingering germs. It's enough to make a housewife smash her blender.

Hand Sanitizers

Household microbiology doesn't have academic respectability yet, but companies are happy to fund its development. For the most part, the companies try to stay away from the unpleasant side of the subject (or so they claim). Purell is one of the most innovative new products, a waterless, portable "hand sanitizer" mixing alcohol and moisturizer that can be applied to the hands like baby lotion. Purell is made by Gojo Industries of Ohio. It used to be manufactured exclusively for hospitals, nursing homes, and food establishments. Then a few years ago, Gojo got a flood of calls from health care professionals eager to have the product for their personal use, says

Paul Alper, until recently the spokesman for Gojo.

Gojo's new target audience is "anybody with an 'on the go' life-style." By Alper's description, that means an updated Norman Rockwell America: women who want to clean up between diaper changes, or after trips to a fast food joint. Men traveling with kids on weekends to the ball park or picnics or fishing trips. Or, he adds as an aside, professionals eating a sandwich at their desk who can't get to a bathroom to wash their hands, or who are sitting in the window seat of the plane, or who shake lots of hands. Tipper Gore even plugged the product during her frenzy of hand pumping during the [2000] election.

But what are we really talking about here? Harried professionals shuttling around on business trips, eating at their desks, too busy to spare five minutes to go to the bathroom to wash their hands. Politicians doing their tiresome duties. Purell is merely a symptom of a beleaguered, stressed-out life, not an antidote. The advertising campaign does not feature Sunday family outings at Lake Placid. It shows an ominous dark circle at the center of which is either a pair of scissors or a phone receiver. If you look closely, you realize the circle is supposed to be a petri dish under a microscope. The object shown is made up of bunched bacteria surrounded by other floating globs of germs. "What did you pick up today?" reads the caption, and the following text explains: "Germs pop up in surprising places. So chances are you pick up handfuls every day." Purell's television ad starts out focusing on a single germ, then pulls back to reveal it's on an ATM machine, as a narrator says, "Who knows what you're in line for." Alper doesn't see the problem: "We got *Adweek*'s best of the month for that one," he says.

False Advertising

Other companies have gotten in trouble for their ad campaigns. This year [1997], the Environmental Protection Agency [EPA], which regulates pesticides, disciplined at least four companies for misleading advertising. The first was Hasbro, the company that makes Playskool toys. In 1995, Hasbro test-marketed an antibacterial high chair. The chair was made with Microban, a germ killer patented by a North Carolina company. Microban incorporates a substance called triclosan into the polymers of the plastic, and creates a kind of protective coating. Hasbro originally advertised that

the product "protects your child from germs and bacteria." But the
EPA claimed Microban protects the toy, not the child, and fined
Hasbro $120,000. Now the toys say "Microban—built in to pro-
tect the toy; inhibits the growth of bacteria." Hasbro officials are
unrepentant. Spokesman Wayne Charness complained that the fine
was "unwarranted," as he told *The Chicago Tribune* in April
[1997]. "It's a nuance of language. We think we've been making
appropriate claims from the beginning."

Most scientists point to a more basic problem: germs may be
transferred from hard surfaces to hands, but there is no scientific
proof that this mode of transmission of the germ causes infections.
And most infections parents worry about, such as colds and flus,
are caused by viruses, not bacteria. Dr. Elizabeth Scott is another
household microbiologist now working as a food and hygiene consultant in Boston. She is very worried about the home as a source
of disease. But she is also very dubious about the toys. In day care
centers, protecting toys might make sense, but kids at home wal-
low in their own germs and spit them on their siblings. "To put
things in perspective," she says, "I have three children, and they all
go out and start eating dirt. We should focus on where the real risks
are. All this hype doesn't teach consumers much." Microban sup-
porters complain that most scientists don't understand how triclosan works, but that's because the manufacturers don't publish
most of their studies. It's routine for companies to keep innovations
secret, but this secrecy serves mainly to foil critics. If Microban
wants to silence its critics, it should look to Lysol as its model.

Lysol is known among scientists for its thorough studies, published in scientific journals and subjected to peer review. In 1991,
a lab that tests Lysol products chose a day care center on Long Island for an experiment. For the first year, the researchers tracked
infections and illnesses, and counted how many times the children
went to the doctor, or missed school. The second year they subjected the staff to a Microbiology 101 course. They told the teach-
ers to wash the toys with disinfectant, the bus drivers to wipe down
the seats and handrails, and showed the janitorial staff the hot
spots to clean. It was a low-tech, simple solution. And it worked.
Infections dropped by a quarter, respiratory illnesses dropped 37
percent, doctor visits dropped, and the kids missed half as much
school. If Microban had a study like this to show, skeptics would
keep quiet.

Another company disciplined by the EPA is 3M, maker of antibacterial O-Cel-O sponges. Launched in May 1996, the company advertised that the sponge "Kills Germs!" and "Kills Germs that cause food-borne Illness." But then the EPA had to remind the company that the sponge only kills germs in the sponge, and that the most the company could prove was that the sponge didn't smell as bad. Still, 3M didn't learn. In June [1997], Colleen Douglas, of 3M's home care products division, was quoted saying, "it's a fabulous product for the health conscious consumer." Spokeswoman Mary Auvin added, "People would rather use our sponges . . . than measure out bleach and pesticides." But that was precisely the EPA's point! The recommended way to sanitize a kitchen counter is to wipe it down with bleach. A sponge can't protect the counter.

Even Gerba, who did much of the research for 3M, thinks the company's claims might be misleading. "I don't know how long it's effective. The label says hundreds of uses, but I'm not sure what the limit is." Lysol tested an antibacterial sponge, and rejected the idea. "We couldn't find that it had any appreciable benefit," says researcher Joe Rabino. "We had people use them in their homes and found there was still lots of bacteria there. In a consumer's mind, they see 'antibacterial' and think it's killing germs, not just resisting odors. It's misleading."

It's Overkill, but Doesn't Kill All the Bugs

Scientists are most dubious about Farberware's myriad gadgets. Take the pizza cutter. "The cheese may get behind the wheel and drip onto the handle," explains Jeff Siegel, executive vice president. "Pizza cutter!" says an incredulous Dr. Scott. "Why would you need an antibacterial pizza cutter? That is definitely not a high-risk food. The pizza is cooked at such a high temperature it's virtually scorched. This is what I mean by jumping on the bandwagon." To prove their products' effectiveness, Farberware sent me a brief lab report from the ACTS Testing Lab in Buffalo, New York. The report concludes that Microban cutting boards "prevent and eliminate bacterial contamination." But even researchers at ACTS are not sure what that conclusion means. "I don't know how long it lasts," says Laura McKenrick. "They claim it's a lifetime effect, but how can that be when the product keeps leaching out?" Research conditions, she admits, are less than ideal. Companies don't send a board that's been used in a home for two years. "We're lucky if [the manufacturer] drops the product off at our doorstep and needs the results in two days. These are not those very, very involved EPA studies."

After the first few EPA penalties, the makers of Microban have instructed clients to take a standard fallback position. "It doesn't replace good hygiene," says Siegel. "You still have to wash the products. It's just an added measure of protection." Or, in another variation: "It's just another measure of protection," says Glenn Cueman, of Microban. "You still can't disregard other precautions." But this carefully staged retreat only makes matters worse. Dividing daily life into infinite added layers of protection only fuels the paranoia. You could always concoct a scenario where a child might pick up germs from a sponge, or a dish, which might cause infection. Even with laundry loads of bleach and water, Microban, Lysol spray, pizza cutters, and dog beds, a mother could never be completely sure. "The mentality being sold is you have to kill all the bugs," says Bill Jarvis, of the CDC, "and no matter what product you have, you'll never kill all the bugs."

Not a Serious Risk

Antibacterial products are designed to play into that peculiarly American inability to process risk. Taking constant precautions against food-borne illness makes sense for the very old, or the very young, or the immunologically fragile. But for those "on the go" healthy adults, the major disease risks from ordinary contact with ordinary everyday surfaces and substances are basically zero. And if they do catch a bug, it will probably take the form of mild diarrhea or a common cold.

Dr. Philip Tierno, a microbiologist at New York University Medical Center, may deserve the blame for starting the hysteria. A few years ago, he began swabbing taxis, pay phones, movie theater seats, and restaurant chairs—and publishing the results in newspapers. Tierno himself wipes the receivers of public phones with alcohol swabs, uses paper towels to open the doors of rest rooms, and never rides the subway. He has studied Microban products, and has high hopes for them. "I wish the toys had been around when my kids were young," he says.

Tierno does not have high hopes for the press, however. "You probably decided on the story you were going to write before you got here," he tells me. "You will write that while these products have some usefulness, all of these problems can be solved with common-sense solutions, like washing hands." And what would he write? "I would say that yes, while there are perhaps a few products that may escape one's impression of usefulness, there is no doubt as to the efficacy of many of them. They are extra tools, that's all."

Actually, Tierno is wrong on both counts. My advice would be, perhaps, when you are old, and your immune system is shot, cook your hamburgers to 160 degrees and wash your hands for sixty seconds or more. But until then turn on bathroom sinks with your hands, and eat rare meat if you want to. If you get sick, stay home from work, and return two days later. If Tierno thinks you sloth-ful, so be it. He can go eat his sandwich in his bathroom.

Antimicrobial Products Are Necessary

By the Soap and Detergent Association

The Soap and Detergent Association (SDA), along with the Cosmetic, Toiletry, and Fragrance Association (CTFA) and microbiologist Dr. Charles Gerba, published an article to counter the American Medical Association's (AMA's) caution that antimicrobial products may be a cause of drug-resistant bacteria. In this article, excerpted below, Gerba and his associates claim that the caution is based on speculation, and that antimicrobial products provide a necessary extra level of protection for consumers. These products kill or inhibit the growth of disease-causing bacteria; and, obviously, contact with fewer infectious bacteria is healthier. This extra level of protection is just the next step in the natural evolution of the human battle against germs. The authors point out that there is huge public demand for these products, that people are concerned about real bacterial threats, and that the AMA's caution misleads the public about the causes of drug-resistant bugs.

Consumers should continue to use antibacterial personal care/cleaning products in the home with confidence, according to the Cosmetic, Toiletry, and Fragrance Association (CTFA), The Soap and Detergent Association (SDA), and a leading health expert, Dr. Charles Gerba. They were responding to the American Medical Association's (AMA) discussion that could dissuade consumers from using an important defense against disease-causing germs.

Antibacterial Products Are Good

Antibacterial personal care/cleaning products, depending on their formulation and application, kill or inhibit the growth of bacteria that cause skin infections, intestinal illnesses or other commonly transmitted diseases. These include potentially fatal illnesses caused by bacteria such as *Salmonella* and *E. coli.*

"Our society is increasingly concerned about the very real threat of disease caused by bacteria. Fortunately, antibacterial personal-care products provide an extra measure of protection for consumers at home and doctors and nurses in hospitals," said Ed Kavanaugh, President of CTFA, the national trade association representing the cosmetic, toiletry and fragrance industry. "That is why there is such a demand for these products."

The American Medical Association's caution to consumers about using antimicrobial soaps and washes is a mistake, said Dr. Charles Gerba, professor of Environmental Microbiology at the University of Arizona and a world-renowned expert on bacteria.

"It is irresponsible for credible medical professionals to dismiss the entire category of antimicrobial products that fight disease-causing germs based on speculative scientific theories," Dr. Gerba said. "These products dramatically reduce the risk of contracting infections from common bacteria, such as *Salmonella* or *E. coli,* in the home.

"The simplest defense against disease is prevention, and the first defense is always good hygiene," Dr. Gerba added. "And antimicrobial products have been shown to be an essential part of a good hygiene routine."

Consumers Did Not Cause Antibacterial Resistance

The American Medical Association's discussion is based on untested scientific theory, the CTFA said. In speculating on the role of personal-care products in causing antibiotic resistance, the American Medical Association is diverting attention away from the proven causes of antibacterial resistance.

According to the federal Centers for Disease Control and Prevention, doctors write 50 million unnecessary prescriptions for antibiotics each year. It is this over-prescription of drugs—and their misuse by patients—that are the key reasons for the emergence of antibiotic resistance, experts say.

"The tangible solution to this problem of antibiotic resistance is in doctors' hands," Ernie Rosenberg, President of SDA said. "Putting the burden on consumers—and taking away effective defenses against disease-causing bacteria—is not the answer."

Added Dr. Gerba: "Civilization has struggled for thousands of years to fight germs for a reason: Germs are bad and getting sick all the time will not make us healthier or immune to other diseases. The real issue remains the overuse and over-prescription of the antibiotic medicines and their use in animal feed."

Because antibiotic resistance and its causes is a critical public health issue, the industry supports the AMA's call for further research on this issue. Since we regard all consumer health questions as being important, the manufacturers of antibacterial products are conducting additional research to further explore all issues that may have an impact on the use of our products.

Vaccination Is Safe and Necessary

By Karen Hsu

Boston Globe correspondent Karen Hsu wrote the following article about childhood vaccinations. Although some parents and activists resist the requirement of vaccination, doctors and scientists say that the risks from childhood disease are much greater than any risks from the vaccines themselves. Some parents think that vaccination should be a matter of choice, once the consenting adult is aware of all the possible risks. However, as Hsu notes, unvaccinated children are susceptible to dangerous diseases. Not only might an infected child suffer and perhaps die, but that child may also spread the hazard to other unvaccinated individuals. Parents today have never experienced an epidemic, and some (at least those who oppose vaccination) appear unable to fathom the devastation that an outbreak of a dangerous disease can cause. Many childhood diseases are still a real threat, Hsu contends, even if they are no longer common in the United States. It is only because of vaccination, however, that the incidence has declined, Hsu maintains. And the importation of hazardous diseases from foreign countries where vaccination is an uncommon occurrence is still a deadly threat to the health of America.

Widespread immunization programs have been deemed one of this century's biggest public health successes. Gone are the days when parents kept their children from the movies, the beach, or other crowded areas, mostly in the 1940s and 1950s, for fear that they would be struck down by the fast-moving poliovirus.

Today, vaccination programs have essentially eradicated infectious childhood diseases in industrialized countries.

But many parents of today's children weren't even born when

the threat of disease made childhood disability and death an all too common event. Because they haven't seen the devastation caused by polio, diphtheria, meningitis, rubella, or measles, all of which have been nearly eliminated by vaccines, some are wondering why their children need certain shots and are focusing on the very small risks of side effects that the vaccines carry.

Vaccine Controversies

Parents like Deborah Bermudes of Massachusetts Citizens for Vaccination Choice, whose mailing list includes 1,000 people, say that as more vaccines become mandated, parents should have the right to choose which ones they do and don't want their children to have. Currently, parents must show proof that their children have been vaccinated against certain diseases before the children can enter public or private school. Meanwhile, the government [has added] a pneumococcal vaccine to those that infants already receive.

Vaccination involves exposing the body to either a weakened or killed virus to build immunity to a given disease. Although rare, side effects do occur. For example, several of the vaccines carry a small risk of anaphylactic shock, a serious allergic reaction that causes blood pressure to drop and the heart to beat erratically. And there are stories of children developing long-term neurological damage from vaccines, such as autism or multiple sclerosis, but it is not clear if vaccines were really the culprit. And although exceedingly rare, a handful of children develop paralysis from the polio vaccine each year.

Bermudes believes that vaccinations, "like all other nonemergency medical procedures, should be subject to informed consent."

The newest mandated vaccines . . .—one for hepatitis B . . . and for chicken pox (*Varicella*) . . .—have caused controversy among parents because some believe that these vaccines, in particular, are causing neurological problems, and some refuse to get their children vaccinated.

Weighing Risk Appropriately

Parents may see chicken pox as a mild disease, but a small percentage of people infected with chicken pox develop severe pneumonia or brain infections from the disease. Children with chicken pox are also at greater risk of developing serious "flesh-eating" streptococcal infections, said Dr. Sean Palfrey, director of the immunization initiative for the Massachusetts chapter of the American Academy of Pediatrics and a pediatrician at Boston Medical Center.

Out of the 4 million people infected with chicken pox each year, 11,000 have to be hospitalized and 100 of them die. "People forget that when someone says 'I want choice,' his child may be the 1 in 10 with bad chicken pox," Palfrey said.

Denise Kretz of Milton [Massachusetts] wanted her two young children to get chicken pox the natural way: from other kids. She was so adamant about it that she joined a network of parents who hosted "chicken pox parties"; when one child got the disease, the parents invited other children over to get exposed to it, since exposure confers lifelong immunity. Nationally, about 1 percent of children are given exemptions from immunizations because of medical, religious, or philosophical reasons. However, it was a religious exemption in Massachusetts that led to the death of a four-year-old in 1994 who contracted diphtheria, the only US case that year; it is not known how the child contracted the disease. Still, Massachusetts, Maine, and Vermont, where children can get some or all of the exemptions, have some of the highest vaccination compliance rates in the country.

Dr. Samuel Katz, a pediatrician at Duke University, said he understands parents' concerns about vaccines and frankly tells them that everything has some risk—from getting vaccines to taking antibiotics. But Katz said that in the past 30 years, he has seen only six children who had serious reactions to vaccines while he's more commonly seen such reactions to antibiotics.

"More people are struck by lightning than by vaccines," said Katz. Vaccine-preventable diseases such as diphtheria and measles still occur worldwide, so they are "not further than a jet ride away," Katz said. Every case of measles last year in the US was traced to someone who had come from or had visited a foreign country, Katz said.

And now diphtheria is only a jet ride away. While the US has had few cases of diphtheria for many years, Russia saw 2,000 cases occur when diphtheria immunization dipped because of the recent collapse of its public health infrastructure.

The US got a wake-up call between 1989 and 1991 when measles inoculations lapsed among preschool children in some urban areas. During those three years, 55,000 people got sick and

120 died, most of them children under 5.

The most recent evidence of how a vaccination has wiped out a serious disease is the *Haemophilus influenzae* type B (Hib) vaccine first introduced in the US in 1990. At the time, Hib was the most common cause of bacterial meningitis, an inflammation of the covering of the brain and spinal cord, accounting for more than 15,000 cases and between 400 to 500 deaths a year. Since the vaccine's development (it's now given routinely to all infants), Hib meningitis has dropped to fewer than 50 cases a year.

But Denise Kretz of Milton, who wanted her children to get exposed to chicken pox through "chicken pox parties," didn't get that opportunity with her youngest son, Bobby, who is almost two. After he received the chicken pox vaccine, he suffered seizures from the inoculation, according to doctors at the New England Medical Center's Floating Hospital for Children. A year later, Bobby still loses his balance often, falls frequently, and cannot talk, even though he could speak when he got the vaccine.

Tracking Adverse Effects

Peter Wintheiser of Easthampton [Massachusetts], said that he believes that his son Billy, now 10, became autistic as a result of a measles/mumps/ rubella shot he got when he was 18 months old. At the time, Wintheiser was a nurse working for Pennsylvania's health department and had given hundreds of thousands of immunizations himself. Nine days after getting the shot, Billy had a seizure and stopped breathing. Over the next few months, he lost his ability to speak and was diagnosed as autistic. "I am convinced that he is autistic because of the vaccine," Wintheiser said. "We have gotten a number of doctors to say that it could be related, which isn't the same as it is."

When he was working at the public health department, Wintheiser reported his child's and other children's side effects to a national reporting system run jointly by the US Food and Drug Administration and the Centers for Disease Control and Prevention (CDC). In 1986, a reporting system was set up for parents and doctors to report vaccine-related injuries and an injury compensation fund for families was begun.

The Vaccine Adverse Effect Reporting System (VAERS) receives about 1,000 reports a month. Gina Mootrey, CDC medical epidemiologist and VAERS project officer, said that while only a limited number of adverse events are mandated for reporting by vaccine providers and manufacturers, "we encourage the reporting of any event felt to be clinically significant either by the parent of the vaccinee or healthcare provider," Mootrey said.

"We try to tell physicians that they don't have to believe that the vaccine caused the event for it to be reported," Mootrey said. She said that the more reports they get, the easier it will be to see if real patterns emerge so that vaccines can be reevaluated if necessary. "If the reports never get sent in, we have no way of knowing we need to look at them." For example, a parent reported to a pediatrician that her child experienced hair loss after each dose of the hepatitis vaccine. A search on the VAERS database found 45 cases of hair loss after hepatitis B vaccination.

Improving Vaccines

Experts point to the rotavirus vaccine when reassuring parents about safety. A vaccine against rotavirus, the leading cause of severe childhood diarrhea, was pulled off the market in 1999 after it was determined that it carried the risk of causing a rare but dangerous bowel obstruction.

Researchers and physicians say they are constantly looking at ways to improve vaccines. One that has long been scrutinized and considered to be problematic is the pertussis (whooping cough) vaccine.

A recent Canadian study of the newest pertussis vaccine (DTaP) showed the most disturbing side effects, such as seizures, have declined sharply since the introduction of a new "acellular" version that includes only the "safe" parts of the germ responsible for the disease.

The older "whole-cell" vaccine had been a catalyst for immunization opponents; seizures and collapse occurred in one per 1,750 injections.

"The message to parents is: 'The bad vaccine is gone,'" said Dr. David Scheifele, study author and director of the Vaccine Evaluation Center at Children's Hospital in British Columbia.

Vaccination Is Risky and Unnecessary

By Marnie Ko

Marnie Ko is an investigative reporter who specializes in crime and law, human interest stories, society and culture, and controversies. She has published in many Canadian newspapers and magazines. In the following article for the Canadian national newsmagazine *The Report*, Ko presents evidence to counter the public health claim that mass vaccination is necessary for community and global health. Activists who document that vaccinations result in numerous, life-altering side effects, Ko reports, have had to battle the pharmaceutical companies who profit so much from these vaccines. Ko points out that these are the same companies that perform most of the clinical trials for approval of vaccines. Aside from the profiteering involved in vaccination programs, at least one researcher contends that vaccines only control a specific form of a disease and not its mutated variants, and that vaccines modify the immune system and may be responsible for the increase of chronic allergic and autoimmune disorders such as diabetes. With confidence in the medical community and pharmaceutical companies waning, Ko insists that statements such as these seem plausible to some, if not many, parents.

G rowing numbers of parents and medical experts question the merits of mass immunization. . . . Evidence of a grass-roots mutiny against the vaccination army has been popping up everywhere. Articles in the *American Spectator, Reason* magazine, the *Washington Post, Insight, The Next City* and elsewhere have been openly sceptical of inoculations. ABC's *20/20* aired a program critical of public health orthodoxy [in 1999]. Dozens of Internet sites have sprung up from anti-vaccine groups in Canada, the U.S. and New Zealand, threatening to over turn the medical orthodoxy that vaccinations have almost single-handedly eliminated killer plagues and scourges that once terrorized the planet. Many of them detail the tragedies of children damaged or killed after having had routine childhood shots, and they delve into major lawsuits launched against vaccine manufacturers. Growing numbers of medical experts, too, are citing scientific studies and questioning the safety of shots, the intentions of the pharmaceutical giants that make them, and the public health benefits of mass vaccination. . . .

Vaccines Are Profitable

Hundreds of millions of dollars in profit are at stake for the pharmaceutical companies which develop and market the shots. The anti-vaccine dissent comes just as pharmaceutical companies are spending billions researching and developing more than 200 new vaccines for everything from AIDS to pregnancy. The average [Canadian or American] child already receives [more than 20] vaccination doses for [at least 10] different diseases by [the start of school], and [several] more before completing high school. . . . [Varivax, the chicken pox vaccine developed by Merck Frosst Pharmaceuticals, is one of the newer ones.]

Chicken pox is a highly infectious disease that most children get. Undoubtedly unpleasant, it is considered benign and, once had, is not usually contracted again. The older a person is when they get it, the more severe the illness.

American Varivax magazine ads warn parents that "40 American children die each year of chicken pox." (About the same number get hit by lightning.) Merck Frosst spokeswoman Christine Homsy says that the company doesn't intend to use such "scare tactics" [in Canada]. Rather, the vaccine is being sold using a cost-benefit analysis, accounting the lost wages of parents who stay home with a sick child. But no one knows how long the shot's protection against disease lasts, so a baby immunized at 12 months might be vulnerable again at age 25, with significantly higher risks. "That's always a problem when you introduce a new vaccine," concedes Dr. Waters. "But we can [always] introduce a booster dose."

Some Vaccines Are Ludicrous for Children

Many more vaccines for preventable, lifestyle diseases contracted largely through risky behaviours (such as herpes, chlamydia and cocaine addiction) are in the pipeline, too. Researcher Peter Cohen, formerly at the National Institute of Drug Abuse, argued in 1996 that cocaine addiction could be analogized to an "infectious disease." If a vaccine for cocaine addiction followed the trend of the hepatitis B vaccination, it would become part of the routine set of vaccinations administered to all children—in case they become cocaine users.

The hepatitis B vaccine itself has provoked widespread debate. Launched in 1982, it initially targeted groups at high risk for the disease that is transmitted by direct exchange of blood and bodily fluids: IV drug users, homosexuals and prostitutes. Today, in the U.S., it is routinely given to babies two months old and is mandated for all daycare children. Forty-two states require children to receive the hepatitis B vaccine to attend school. In Canada, the shots are voluntary and offered to teenagers at school, though Health Canada officials have recommended all babies and children be inoculated. Clinical trials for the vaccines, made by Smith Kline Beecham and Merck Sharp and Dohme Canada, however, only involved healthy adults who were monitored for just four to five days after the shots. . . .

Critics charge that giving needless shots to children to pacify parental hysteria is poor public health policy. Kristine Severyn, director of the Ohio-based Vaccine Policy Institute, thinks such policies are fuelled less by good science than "big money" and "politics." So is the growing inclination of health officials to treat every problem with a vaccine, she adds. And with each new vaccine on the market, parents grow increasingly vulnerable. "Parents who opt their children out of vaccine schedules are considered child abusers," says Mrs. Severyn, who holds a doctorate in biopharmaceutics and toxicology.

The Supervaccine

Meanwhile, vaccine manufacturers are working on a Holy Grail of inoculations: the supervaccine. Researchers are asking the world's governments for $500 million to develop a genetically engineered supervaccine which will contain raw DNA from 20 to 30 viruses, parasites and bacteria. The shot would deliver a time-released vaccine that would insert itself directly into an infant's cells over a period of time, containing a smorgasbord of viruses including the most feared: HIV, diphtheria, malaria, pneumonia, meningitis, polio, typhoid fever, and tuberculosis. Scientists note this vaccine poses extreme risks, because it could not be "recalled" if a child suffered adverse reactions.

More Risk than Just Direct Side Effects

A growing number of medical experts maintain these are just a few of the problems with mass vaccination. Some researchers say immunization programs only appear to eradicate a disease, but in actuality present an opportunity for the disease to reappear later—this time in a mutated, more dangerous form, affecting age groups not previously at risk of the disease. Denver, Colorado, physician Philip Incao has served as a medical expert for families with vaccine-damaged children. Last year [1999], he testified at a U.S. congressional hearing about yet another vaccine concern: the frequency of acute and chronic adverse effects of vaccines are far greater than officially acknowledged. Dr. Incao added that although vaccines may prevent the onset of a particular illness, they modify the immune system and "increase the tendency to chronic allergic and auto-immune reactions." He cited recent research that linked some vaccines to auto-immune diseases, especially diabetes. Other researchers point out that vaccines contain known toxic and carcinogenic chemicals, viruses, bacteria and bacterial toxins, and human- and animal-derived host tissues. These vaccine components are inherently hazardous and can cause disease, disability and death, they maintain. Others are bothered by the use of aborted fetuses in developing certain vaccines.

Confidence in vaccinations has always been based on the medical community's contention that inoculation is the safest and most effective way to prevent disease. Public health officials do not deny that serious side effects and deaths occur from the shots. They do, however, downplay their severity, fearing that any suggestion of risks may lead parents to reject vaccinations altogether. Health Canada's Vaccine Adverse Events Reporting System receives between 4,000 and 5,000 voluntary case reports per year. It is suspected that thousands more go unreported. Parents are assured, with the arrival of each new vaccine, that the product has been subjected to rigorous tests before approval. Health Canada says the "requirements for licensing vaccines in Canada are stringent and ensure that excellent research into potential adverse effects has been conducted prior to widespread use. No long-term effects have been associated with any vaccine currently in use."

Vaccine Testing Is Questionable

However, late last year the Association of American Physicians and Surgeons (AAPS) demanded a congressional investigation of the vaccine testing and approval process. Typically, a vaccine is manufactured and tested in the U.S., approved by the U.S. Food and Drug Administration, and eventually introduced into Canada. So Canadians had a reason to be concerned when the rotavirus vaccine (aimed at preventing diarrhea in young infants) was abruptly pulled off the U.S. market after just one year. When 15 cases of infants suffered life-threatening intestinal obstructions after the shot, AAPS accused the Food and Drug Administration and the Centers for Disease Control of ignoring or concealing data that recorded problems from the outset. What's more, the AAPS charged that the rate of intestinal obstruction found in clinical trials before FDA granted approval were alarming. One investigation revealed 30 times the expected rate of the deadly condition.

Neither parents nor doctors were warned to watch for symptoms, and the CDC website says only that rotavirus had been "associated with mild problems." In fact, eight infants required surgery, and one lost seven inches of bowel. The rotavirus vaccine has now been recalled.

"We have to wonder whether the rotavirus story is the tip of the iceberg," says Tucson, Arizona, physician Jane Orient, executive director of the AAPS. She questions the safety and integrity of the testing process. "We believe it may be tainted by conflicts of interest in the United States and Canada," she says.

According to Dr. Orient, a conflict is presented by vaccine studies, which are almost always funded by the pharmaceutical companies which manufacture the shots. "These incestuous ties are susceptible to corruption," she says. Vaccines carry risks of "fatal or complicated side effects including brain damage, particularly the pertussis vaccine," Dr. Orient warns. According to the prominent doctor, parents' concerns are well placed. "Vaccines have not been investigated with the intensity they should have been. Now, a whole generation is being subjected to shots with no idea of the outcome, and even more are on the way," she notes.

In addition to limited testing, vaccines are often recalled after they have been administered to children. For example, the American Pediatric Association has recently admitted a plausible link between the oral polio vaccine and polio outbreaks. It has now reversed its long-held earlier position and wants to vaccinate American children by injection instead. Meanwhile, the oral vaccine is still used in Third World countries. Single doses of measles and mumps vaccines are now banned in Britain, though just a few years ago public health officials zealously defended their safety record. It is all too common, according to Dr. Orient, for vaccines to be quietly taken off the market with as little attention paid to the recall as possible.

Parents Are Exposing Faults in the System

Accountability is an issue, agrees Catherine Diodati, a Canadian researcher based in Ontario. Ms. Diodati, author of the 1999 book, *Immunization, History, Ethics, Law and Health*, says long-term studies on vaccines are not conducted. When studies are done at all, "the methodology used is highly questionable." Two groups using different multiple vaccines usually substitute for an unvaccinated control group in studies of adverse events, says Ms. Diodati. Her interest in vaccinations began 14 years ago, after her then six-month-old daughter fell unconscious for an entire week after her third DPT shot. "She began crying and could not be consoled. It continued for hours. Then, my normally bright and responsive baby stopped responding altogether," recalls Ms. Diodati, who immediately called the doctor. "He told me [the baby's] reaction could not possibly be associated with the vaccine. He became defensive and dismissed me as a 'hysterical mother,' and insisted I continue to bring the baby in for further immunizations." Instead, Ms. Diodati embarked on her book to counter "public health propaganda."

The greatest threat to future mass vaccination programs and the integrity of public health may well be books like Ms. Diodati's, as well as modern communication tools like the Internet. Still, in the face of damaging anti-vaccination literature, public health officials continue promoting immunizations as "the most important interventions to prevent disease ever discovered." "To have a tool as valuable as vaccines and not use it is considered unconscionable," is Health Canada's advice for health workers encountering dubious parents.

If the vaccine army is successful, the next decade will see children embark on a scientific experiment without precedent in history. At least one expert thinks the result may bring more grief than good. Says Dr. Orient: "There really is such a thing as too much of a good thing."

Disease Eradication Programs Are the Ultimate Public Health Concern

By Bruce Aylward

Dr. Bruce Aylward was a medical officer for the World Health Organization's (WHO's) Expanded Program on Immunization, and he now is the coordinator for the WHO's Global Polio Eradication Initiative. In 2001, he described the efforts of this initiative, which began in 1988, in the following article. Originally, the goal of the Polio Initiative was for eradication by 2000, but that has been pushed back to 2005, with confirmation of eradication through 2008 and ideally cessation of immunizations in 2009 and later. The disease is currently endemic in only six countries, but cultural and political resistance in some of these areas has led to increased outbreaks that have spread to other countries. The final push to eliminate polio is critical to prevent the reappearance of polio in countries that are now free of it. Aylward believes that disease eradication programs are the ultimate goal for public health, and that they bring universal benefits to every person vaccinated against such diseases.

T hough we live in an age of conservation, the deliberate extinction of an ancient life form is being relentlessly pursued worldwide with increasing zeal. Encouraged by political leaders, financed by a coalition of industry, governments, private benefactors, and celebrities, but operating largely out of sight of the media, an army of professionals and volunteers has already eliminated this organism from over 175 countries. The world is standing by, not to mourn the senseless obliteration of yet another member of the earth's living heritage, but to celebrate the consignment to history of a disease that until recently was one of the world's most dreaded illnesses. Only 10 years ago, the poliovirus was paralyzing 1,000 children every day; today it is on the verge of being eradicated forever. Now, however, the greatest threat to delivering a polio-free world to future generations is complacency in the face of this disappearing disease.

Disease eradication has been described as the ultimate goal in public health. It entails not just the reduction of the target pathogen to zero, but also the eventual cessation of all control measures against it. While the humanitarian arguments for pursuing the eradication of an organism are compelling in themselves, the full benefits of these initiatives go far beyond the permanent elimination of a disease.

Eradication is also good economics. Though the ongoing global effort to eradicate polio will cost US$2.5 billion over 20 years, these costs pale against the US$1.5 billion that the world stands to save every year in direct costs alone once immunization efforts can stop.

Requirements for Eradication

Although at first glance eradication appears to be an elegant, cost-effective solution for tackling the diseases that plague mankind, few organisms are actually amenable to this solution. We lack the tools, resources, and commitment to launch and ensure the success of eradication initiatives against most pathogens. In general, an organism can only be eradicated if humans are essential to its life cycle, if there is no reservoir other than humans, and if it has no chronic carrier state. Thus, while HIV/AIDS, tuberculosis, and malaria together claim more than four million lives every year, not to mention the economic toll they exact, these diseases are not at present candidates for eradication.

Once a disease has met the biological criteria needed to be considered "eradicable," there must be an effective tool, whether a vaccine, drug, or other intervention, to efficiently interrupt transmission of the pathogen among humans. Even then the benefit of applying these tools in a massive eradication campaign must outweigh the financial, human, and other opportunity costs of such an effort. In addition, there must be social and political recognition of the value of seeking eradication, rather than just pursuing ongoing control of the disease. Perhaps most importantly, this commitment must be sustainable over the 10 to 20 years that will be required to implement the program. Such commitment is especially important and particularly difficult to secure during the final phase of an eradication initiative, when the target disease is rapidly disappearing and when the marginal costs of delivering the program are skyrocketing.

Even when the rigorous criteria outlined above are met, eradication remains a high-risk enterprise. Of the six initiatives that have been launched to eradicate a human pathogen in the last 100 years, three failed outright, two have yet to conclude, and only one has been unreservedly successful. Certification of the eradication of smallpox in 1980, with the rapid cessation of immunization against that disease, continues to stand as the only testament to humanity's capacity to successfully and permanently eliminate a disease that has plagued it throughout history.

The early eradication initiatives of this century targeting yellow fever, malaria, and yaws, a disease now confined to Africa, were fatally flawed from the outset due to an incomplete understanding of the biology of these diseases at the time. In contrast, the technical feasibility of the ongoing initiatives to eradicate poliomyelitis (launched in 1988 and scheduled for completion in 2005) and dracunculiasis, or Guinea worm, has already been demonstrated by the elimination of both organisms from at least four continents. Ironically, now the greatest challenge is ensuring the financial resources and political commitment to accelerate eradication activities through the [final years].

Logistics of Eradication

Someone once remarked that the solution to eradicating a particular disease amongst cattle was straightforward enough—simply have all the cows stand in the same place for 24 hours. Though facetious, the comment strikes an uncanny note of truth in underscoring the logistical challenges to implementing a global eradication effort, no matter how simple the tool or strategy for delivering it.

Polio proves the point. The necessary tool for its eradication is
an oral vaccine that can be safely administered to a child by anyone with a few minutes of simple instruction. In 2000 alone, however, applying this tool to eradicate polio required the immunization of 550 million children by 10 million people in 85 countries.
Every one of these 10 million volunteers had to be identified,
trained, supplied, and supported to deliver an extremely heat-
sensitive vaccine to children everywhere, even to those living in
the midst of areas of armed conflict. To optimize the impact of
their work, these volunteers also needed to be coordinated, as the
activity was completed over one to three days in each country. For
example, in India 147 million children were immunized on December 6, 2000.

Not all eradication efforts require an effort on the scale of the
National Immunization Days conducted against polio. The scale
of effort depends on the target disease, its geographic distribution,
and the tool being used to interrupt its transmission. Regardless
of the scale of the effort, though, all eradication initiatives have
depended on an extensive use of community volunteers. The reasons for this are twofold. First, the scale of eradication campaigns
is usually too large to be delivered solely through the traditional
health infrastructure and networks. Second, the last refuge of most
diseases that are targeted for eradication are those geographic areas where health services are weakest, if not altogether absent.

Predictably, these "chronically unreached" populations pose
some of the greatest challenges to ongoing disease eradication efforts, just as they have in the past. The last case of smallpox in a
child occurred in a remote area in the Horn of Africa. In a keynote
address to the polio-eradication partnership in September 2000.
UN Secretary-General Kofi Annan asked the audience to try to
picture the last child that might ever be paralyzed by polio: "He
or she is probably under five, probably living in Africa, possibly
in the midst of hunger, poverty, or armed conflict. Our race to
reach this child is a race against time."

Reaching children in conflict-ridden areas poses a special challenge, but also a unique opportunity. The need to implement polio-
immunization campaigns has been used to negotiate a cessation
of hostilities, at least temporarily, in countries such as Peru, Sri
Lanka, the Philippines, Afghanistan, Somalia, the Democratic Republic of the Congo, and Sierra Leone. These opportunities, however small or short-lived, have definitely contributed to the design

and implementation of other health interventions for these populations and have often encouraged the larger peace-building efforts that were under way.

Unusual Alliances

Disease eradication has been described as the ultimate in health equity and social justice because these campaigns bring identical and universal benefits to every person, everywhere. For example, if all children are to share the benefits of a polio-free world in perpetuity, every child must be reached with the polio vaccine.

Given the uneven distribution of financial wealth and technical expertise in the world, the human and financial resources needed to implement eradication strategies are often only found far from the site of the target disease. Polio had long disappeared from industrialized countries by the time the global eradication initiative was launched. Had key decision-makers in these countries not been old enough to have experienced the terror of polio in their communities in the pre-vaccine era, it is unlikely that the necessary US$2.5 billion in external financing could ever have been mobilized. That these decision-makers have supported the polio-eradication initiative is largely due to the efforts of Rotary International, a private-sector public-service organization, which has diligently lobbied governments for financial support. Rotary's success is in part due to its own credibility, having raised over US$500 million for the initiative from its 1.2 million members worldwide.

The chronic challenge of fund-raising for a disease that is virtually unknown in the West has on several occasions nearly undone the eminently achievable goal of Guinea worm eradication. Even in countries where the disease is endemic, it is often very difficult to secure political support for its eradication, as its incidence is limited to the most destitute rural populations. How does one secure US$1 billion to free some of the world's most disenfranchised populations from a cruel, painful, and debilitating disease? One answer is the enlistment of high-profile, tireless advocates such as former US President Jimmy Carter, who has been essential in keeping Guinea worm eradication on the agenda of both development agencies and affected countries.

Even when the necessary financing and human resources are available, getting them to the right place at the right time poses additional challenges. UN agencies, using novel mechanisms such as Interagency Coordinating Committees, have been critical in ensuring that all states, whatever their status, can access the hard currency and technical expertise they need. Specialized technical agencies like the World Health Organization (WHO) have provided international forums to allow the sharing of lessons, strategies, and progress across every country; these agencies have also fostered international acceptance of standard indicators for monitoring performance. Similarly, UN implementing agencies like the UN Children's Fund (UNICEF) have been essential for supporting countries in the implementation of necessary strategies in the field. Were such supranational coordinating and support mechanisms not available through the United Nations, it is questionable whether global eradication initiatives could ever have been launched, let alone successfully implemented.

Hidden Challenges

Of the endless problems that confront an eradication initiative over its lifespan, few, other than a chronic funding gap, are predictable at the outset. Because eradication programs must operate across virtually all cultures and languages over an extended period, it is impossible to plan for all contingencies.

It is unlikely that anyone involved in the early planning of the smallpox initiative anticipated that eradication would threaten to deprive a Hindu goddess of her function as a deity for sufferers of the disease, or that clans in the Horn of Africa would vociferously object to the immunization containment strategy. Only the timely transfer of the goddess's responsibility to other maladies in India and the armed enforcement of the strategies in Ethiopia allowed eradication activities to proceed in those places.

Although armed conflict has always been a prevalent and unfortunate feature in man's history, the remarkable change in the nature of conflict in the latter half of the 20th century has had substantial implications for the feasibility of current and future eradication initiatives. Wars have shifted from being primarily time-limited, interstate affairs to chronic, seemingly unsolvable civil conflicts. As recently as 1988, when the polio-eradication effort was launched, much of Afghanistan, the Democratic Republic of the Congo (then Zaire), Somalia, Sudan, and even parts of Angola were readily accessible. Though the polio strategies are now be-

ing implemented in most areas of these countries, intrastate conflicts will continue to pose some of the greatest challenges to the
ultimate success of this eradication initiative.

Even the evolving political and social priorities of industrialized nations can wreak havoc on an eradication program. In 1988
it would have been impossible to predict that the polio campaign
might eventually be threatened by the lobbying efforts of animal-
rights groups. Since the early 1990s such groups have successfully
lobbied many American and European airlines to prevent the ship-
ment of African green monkeys from breeding colonies in the Car-
ibbean to vaccine-manufacturing sites in Europe. If the demands
of such groups were fully met, the operational feasibility of the
entire eradication initiative could be hampered by a rapidly escalating vaccine price.

When to End an Eradication Program

By definition, an eradication initiative has only been truly successful once all control measures against the target disease have
been stopped. More simply, just as the rescinding of all international smallpox vaccination requirements by the WHO signaled
the ultimate success of that initiative, immunization against polio
must eventually stop if the full benefits of this initiative are to be
realized.

Fifty years ago scientists and politicians often argued over when
and how to introduce polio vaccines into human populations. Scientists are now arguing over when and how to stop using polio
vaccines in human populations. With the disease still found in 20
countries, yet another group is arguing that it is premature even to
discuss the cessation of polio immunization. Although at first
glance it would appear that the simplest aspect of an eradication
program would be stopping it, an analysis of the issues surrounding the cessation of polio immunization highlights the complexity of this issue.

Establishing international consensus on the disease-free status
of countries requires transparent performance monitoring and comparison of data worldwide. For the purposes of polio eradication,
the WHO monitors every country's capacity to detect and investigate paralyzed children, an indicator of poliovirus circulation. Standard indicators allow the comparison of data between countries as
disparate as Afghanistan and Albania, China and Cameroon. These

same indicators and performance standards serve as the basis for certifying regions as polio-free by independent commissions convened for that purpose.

More complex is eradicating poliovirus from the world's laboratories. In areas that are now polio-free, the inadvertent release of a poliovirus from a laboratory could pose a greater risk than an imported virus from a polio-infected area. That the last smallpox death in the world occurred in a medical institution in Birmingham, England, is a vivid reminder of the need to contain laboratory stocks of poliovirus. Learning this lesson from smallpox, the WHO has already established, with broad public consultation, the Global Action Plan for Laboratory Containment of Wild Polioviruses. While the logistics of global containment are complex, with literally tens of thousands of institutions holding wild polioviruses or wild-poliovirus-infected material, progress in the Western Pacific and in Europe demonstrates its feasibility.

The need for global certification and containment prior to the cessation of control measures is common to all eradication initiatives. A recent polio outbreak on the island of Hispaniola, however, underlined yet another issue for those planning the eventual cessation of polio immunization. Investigation of the outbreak found that it had not been caused by a naturally occurring wild poliovirus, but rather by a strain of the vaccine itself. As the oral polio vaccine is in fact made from a weakened version of the wild poliovirus, scientists have always been aware of the theoretical potential for such an outbreak. The Hispaniola outbreak showed that for the polio initiative to be completely successful, however, once all wild strains had been eradicated it would be necessary to ensure the vaccine strains were as well. Given the rarity of events such as the Hispaniola outbreak, the management of this problem will be straightforward, but not without substantial additional cost, time, and international consensus-building.

What Is Next?

Future candidates for disease eradication will face much greater scrutiny and evaluation to determine whether the biological and technical determinants, potential costs and benefits, and societal and political considerations warrant launching an eradication effort. A recent international conference in Atlanta, Georgia, considered a large number of candidates for eradication. The resulting list was very short. No bacterial or parasitic diseases were judged to be eradicable using existing tools, though in the longer term a couple of important organisms might be candidates, given the rapid advance of science and the development of technological tools.

Among the many viral diseases considered, measles, rubella, hepatitis B, and hepatitis A were determined to be biologically and technically feasible candidates for eradication. Measles led the list because there is no reservoir for the virus besides man, the vaccine is very effective, and available diagnostic tools are of sufficient sensitivity and specificity. Furthermore, experience in the Americas suggested that eradication is technically feasible with existing vaccines, but that a coordinated global effort would be needed over a relatively short period of time. Given that measles kills nearly one million children every year, justifying the value of an eradication effort in terms of costs and benefits would probably be relatively straightforward. Because virtually all of the one million measles deaths occur in developing countries, the biggest challenge would be ensuring social and political support for the strategies in industrialized countries. Such challenges were felt to be even more daunting for eradication efforts against the other potential candidate diseases.

Another important conclusion of the meeting was that none of these initiatives would ever be launched were the world to squander its current opportunity to eradicate polio for lack of sufficient funding or political commitment. With less than 3,500 cases of polio reported worldwide in 2000 and at most 20 countries still harboring the disease, the progress of this initiative over the next few years will be central to decisions about backing any future eradication effort.

Perhaps the greatest risk to future eradication initiatives comes from within the international health community itself. Few issues are more divisive in that community than the ongoing debate as to whether targeted health programs, such as polio and Guinea worm eradication, ultimately enhance or detract from broader efforts to strengthen health systems. Though there is increasing evidence that such programs provide tremendous opportunities for strengthening the delivery of other services, it is clear that these opportunities must be exploited more systematically if this debate is to be resolved.

In a world so steeped in cynicism, there are few examples of outstanding international cooperation toward a common good; even when cooperation occurs, it usually takes many years, if ever, before most of the world's population shares in the benefits. Global disease eradication efforts stand in stark contrast. The ongoing efforts to eradicate polio demonstrate that tremendous obstacles can be overcome and achievements realized when humanity works together for the good of its children everywhere.

Disease Eradication Programs Can Overshadow Other Public Health Concerns

By Donald A. Henderson

Dr. Donald A. Henderson was chief of the World Health Organization's (WHO's) Smallpox Eradication Program. He also served on the Global Commission for the Certification of Smallpox Eradication, which was chaired by Dr. Frank Fenner of the Australian National University. He is now professor emeritus at the Johns Hopkins Bloomberg School of Public Health. In 1999, Henderson published the following reflections about the smallpox eradication campaign and what the lessons from that and similar campaigns should teach the public and medical community. He points out that amid the success of smallpox vaccinations were several failed eradication attempts and many unforeseen challenges. However, the campaigns have led to new methods of global surveillance, innovations in the organization of large-scale public health programs, new research, and the delivery of multiple immunizations to children around the world through the expanded program of immunization (EPI). These improvements and lessons can be used to improve many aspects of public health and should not be applied only to narrow global eradication campaigns. Global public health could benefit greatly if cur-

Donald A. Henderson, "Eradication: Lessons from the Past," *Morbidity and Mortality Weekly Report*, December 31, 1999.

rent resources are not channeled into the elimination of one disease
at a time.

O n 8 May 1980, the Thirty-third World Health Assembly
declared that smallpox had been eradicated globally. For
the first time in history, mankind had vanquished a disease. It must be borne in mind, however, that this was not the first
attempt at global disease eradication but the fifth. Within a month,
the Fogarty International Center convened a two-day meeting to
explore the question of what diseases should be eradicated next.
This was the first of a series of conferences of which the present
one is the latest. At that first meeting, the list of diseases and conditions nominated ranged from urban rabies to periodontal disease
to leprosy. Some spoke of eradication, others of elimination, and
yet others of the elimination of a disease as a public health problem—however that might be defined. A tumultuous discussion
eventually culminated in the decision that measles, poliomyelitis
and yaws were clearly suitable for at least regional eradication but
that there were many other possible candidates.

Scepticism About Disease Eradication

One sceptical note was made at the symposium by the two introductory speakers—[Dr. Frank Fenner and myself]. They reflected
on the broader applicability of disease eradication from their van-
tage point of nearly 15 years of participation in the just concluded
smallpox eradication campaign. Their basic conclusion, in brief,
was that there was at that time no other suitable candidate for eradication. As they pointed out, smallpox had a number of highly
favourable characteristics which facilitated eradication including
the very heat-stable vaccine which protected with a single dose.
No other disease came close to matching these advantages. Despite this, eradication was achieved by only the narrowest of mar-
gins. Its progress in many parts of the world and at different times
wavered between success and disaster, often only to be decided
by quixotic circumstance or extraordinary performances by field
staff. Nor was support for the programme generous, whatever the
favourable cost-benefit ratios may have been. A number of endemic countries were themselves persuaded only with difficulty
to participate in the programme; the industrialized countries were

reluctant contributors; and, the United Nation's Children's Emergency Fund (UNICEF), so helpful to the prior malaria programme, decided that it wanted nothing to do with another eradication programme and stated that it would make no contributions. Several countries did make donations of vaccine and the West African programme, directed by the US Communicable Disease Center was a critical addition. However, cash donations to the World Health Organization (WHO) during the first 7 years of the smallpox programme, 1967–73, amounted to exactly US$79,500. That is not per year but the total for that entire period.

Moreover, in 1980, support for any new eradication effort seemed especially unlikely since the smallpox eradication programme was then being critically maligned by traditional international health planners. To them, the smallpox campaign epitomized the worst of what they characterized as anachronistic, authoritarian, "top-down" programmes which they saw as anathema to the new "health for all" primary health care initiative.

Given these considerations, it seemed in 1980 to be little more than an interesting academic exercise to debate what next to eradicate. Having offered this view, Henderson was not again invited to the subsequent workshops, task forces, conferences and special committees on eradication which were later convened. Thus, in reflecting on the lessons to be learned from the yaws, malaria and smallpox campaigns, as I was requested to do, I come to the subject afresh and have had the opportunity to reconsider the question of the next steps in eradication, based on a further 17 years of perspective.

Failed Eradication Efforts

As a reminder, the yaws and malaria campaigns began more or less at the same time, about 1955, and were effectively terminated some 15 years later, in 1970 or soon thereafter. The launch of each was triggered by the introduction of a new technology—an injectable single-dose long-acting penicillin, for the treatment of yaws, and the availability of large quantities of the inexpensive insecticide DDT, for use in the malaria programme. Surprisingly, prior to the launch, neither campaign could draw on the experience of large-scale pilot programmes in critical areas which would have served to demonstrate the feasibility of eradication, given the tools and resources available. If they had, neither programme would have been initiated. The existence of such prior experience would seem to be axiomatic before deciding on any eradication initiative. Yet, even the Dahlem Conference's otherwise commendable review of lessons provided by past eradication programmes effectively overlooks this fundamental precept.

Of the two programmes, malaria was, by far, the most important and during its 15 years of existence, it accounted for more than one-third of WHO's total expenditures and its 500-person WHO staff dwarfed all other programmes. The USA alone contributed nearly a thousand million dollars to the effort. The yaws campaign, in contrast, was much more modest, was little publicized, and was little known.

The strategy of the yaws programme called for the screening of patients for clinical disease and their treatment with penicillin. In all, some 160 million persons were examined and 50 million were treated in 46 countries. Besides having failed to validate the strategy in pilot studies, the programme had two glaring deficiencies. First was the fact that, for the first 10 years of its history, there was no surveillance and so it was not clear as to what was actually happening. When sample serological surveys were eventually conducted, it was discovered immediately that subclinical infections were far more prevalent than had been recognized, making eradication quite impossible. Second, there was no programme of research and thus no operational studies which might have demonstrated far earlier the futility of this exercise.

Unlike the little known yaws programme, the malaria campaign, during its existence, dominated the international health agenda. This programme was active in many countries in Latin America and South Asia as well as Ethiopia, and consumed a substantial proportion of national health expenditures as well as major inputs from WHO and the US Agency for International Development (USAID). The programme failed, but lessons derived from malaria eradication were central in shaping the smallpox eradication strategy. Three operating principles were of particular importance. First was the relationship of the programme itself to the health services. It was a tenet of the malaria eradication directorate that the programme could not be successful unless it had full support from the highest level of government. This translated into a demand that the director of the programme in each country report directly to the head of government and that the malaria service function as an independent, autonomous entity with its own personnel and its own pay scales. Involvement of the community at large or of persons at the community level was not part of the overall strategy.

Second, all malaria programmes were obliged to adhere rigidly to a highly detailed, standard manual of operations. It mandated, for example, identical job descriptions in every country and even prescribed specific charts to be displayed on each office wall at each administrative level. The programme was conceived and executed as a military operation to be conducted in an identical manner whatever the battlefield. Third, the premise of the programme was that the needed technology was available and that success depended solely on meticulous attention to administrative detail in implementing the effort. Accordingly, research was considered unnecessary and was effectively suspended from the launch of the programme.

The Smallpox Campaign

The smallpox eradication campaign had to function differently. Segregating it as an autonomous entity reporting to the head of state was neither politically acceptable nor financially feasible. With a programme budget of only US$2.4 million per year, there was no hope of underwriting more than a small proportion of personnel and programme costs. The programme necessarily had to function within existing health service structures and had to take advantage of available resources. This, in fact, proved advantageous, as contrary to commonly held belief, underutilized health personnel were abundant in most countries. With motivation and direction, most performed well. It was also discovered that those in the community such as teachers, religious leaders and village elders, could and did make invaluable contributions. Rigid manuals of operations intuitively made little sense given the diverse nature of national health structures and so broad goals with provision for flexibility in achieving them became the accepted mode.

Finally, research initiatives were encouraged at every level. This occurred despite the opposition of senior WHO leadership who insisted that the tools were in hand and the epidemiology was sufficiently well understood and that better management was all that was necessary to eradicate smallpox. Research initiatives included the development of new vaccination devices to replace traditional lancets; field studies, which revealed the epidemiology of the disease to be different from that described in the textbooks and, in consequence, the need for modification of basic operations; the discovery that the duration of vaccine efficacy was far longer than that normally stated, making revaccination much less important; operational research, which facilitated more efficient vaccine delivery and case detection; and studies which demonstrated conclusively that there was no animal reservoir. The principle was to ask again and again, how could this programme be made to operate more efficiently, more effectively. And, indeed, without the fruits of these research efforts, it is highly unlikely that eradication would have succeeded. Even as the last cases were being discovered, a joint Dutch-Indonesian study of a new tissue-culture vaccine was just being completed. We hoped we would not require it, but we were prepared, should it be needed.

From the beginning of the programme, surveillance for smallpox cases was a basic strategy of the campaign. As expected, it proved to be the ultimate quality control measure, the guide to improved operations, and the yardstick of progress. These principles for conduct of an eradication programme remain valid today and, as applied in guinea-worm eradication and in poliomyelitis eradication in the Americas and western Asia, have proved eminently successful.

One might imagine that the subject of which diseases might next be eradicated would have been a primary topic of conversation among the large and talented group of epidemiologists who, through the late 1970s, were engaged in eradicating smallpox. In fact, I can't recall the question ever having been seriously raised or discussed. Actually, the question didn't seem especially relevant. This is not to say that we regarded the eradication of smallpox as an end in itself. Far from it.

International Immunization Programs

At the time the smallpox eradication programme began, only two vaccines—BCG [for tuberculosis] and smallpox—were at all widely used throughout the developing world. Few countries had organized national vaccination programmes and those that did, seldom extended much beyond the larger towns and cities; substandard and/or poorly preserved vaccines were in common use; information about disease incidence was woefully inadequate, and effective supervision was generally poor to nil.

Conceptually, as we envisaged it, an effective campaign required the development of a management structure extending from the capital city to the furthest villages; it required that mechanisms be established to assure that fully potent and stable vaccine was used; and that plans be implemented within the existing health service structure to assure its distribution throughout the country to reach at least 80% of the inhabitants. It demanded that a national surveillance system be established, which was at that time an unknown entity in most countries; and it required that planning be done and goals established to reach a finite end-point within a given period. Most national health ministries had never before attempted an effort of this type. It seemed to us that a successful programme would provide valuable training and experience for health service staff and, most important, would create a skeleton framework permitting other activities to be added. Additional vaccines were obviously a logical further step.

In some countries, the simultaneous vaccination with two antigens began soon after the beginning of the programme. In the 20 countries of western and central Africa assisted by CDC, all countries administered smallpox and measles vaccines; in a number of countries of eastern Africa, BCG and smallpox vaccine began to be administered at the same time; and in some countries at special risk, yellow fever vaccine was also added. Few developing countries, however, provided DPT, measles or poliovirus vaccine.

With expansion of the immunization programme in mind, WHO organized, in 1970, an international meeting to review the status of vaccination internationally and to recommend model programmes. Recommended for general use in the developing countries were smallpox, BCG, DPT, measles and typhoid vaccines. Yellow fever and poliovirus vaccines were recommended for use but only under special circumstances. At that time, poliovirus vaccine was not generally recommended because of uncertainty as to how serious a problem poliomyelitis really was for most developing countries and because of doubts as to how efficacious poliovirus vaccine would prove to be in tropical areas. In 1974, this expanded programme of immunization [EPI] was approved by the World Health Assembly; in 1977, programme leadership was strengthened and the programme began to grow. By then, typhoid vaccine had been dropped from the recommended list and poliovirus vaccine was added.

From the eradication of smallpox from 31 endemic countries to the implementation of effective immunization programmes for six diseases in more than 100 countries represents an enormous increase in programme complexity. Nevertheless, remarkable progress has been made in expanding and intensifying immunization activities throughout the world.

In 1990, this culminated in the World Summit for Children and the nominal achievement of the goal of vaccinating 80% of the world's children against six major diseases.

One component of that programme which lagged significantly was surveillance. Not all the EPI diseases lend themselves readily to national surveillance but this did appear feasible, at least for neonatal tetanus, poliomyelitis and measles. However, persuading governments and health workers, whether national or international, that surveillance is as vital for disease control as for eradication proved to be a formidable task. In fact, until 1985, little progress was made.

At that time, Ciro de Quadros, Director of PAHO's [the Pan American Health Organization's] EPI Program, visualized an approach to spur the development of national surveillance programmes in Latin America. The goal was the eradication of poliomyelitis from the Western Hemisphere. With poliomyelitis eradication having been determined to be technically feasible and, in the Americas, practicable as well, the countries of PAHO endorsed the eradication goal and, in so doing, committed themselves to the development of a hemisphere-wide surveillance effort. Sites reporting suspect cases each week increased from some 500 to more than 20,000. Reporting for acute flaccid paralysis was soon extended to include neonatal tetanus, measles and cholera.

During the course of poliomyelitis eradication in the Americas, new paradigms for community involvement in public health emerged as well as approaches for bringing together public and private sector agencies; national immunization days were demonstrated to be a practicable, often more efficient means for vaccine delivery; new approaches were evolved for the planning and integration of international assistance; a hemisphere-wide laboratory network was created; and new mechanisms for vaccine purchase, utilizing PAHO and UNICEF administrative channels, were established. Poliomyelitis eradication was the visible target of the programme but the agenda was far broader than this and the accomplishments likewise.

With this further background of experience, what now might I offer as lessons to the future? In contemplating this question, it is important to bear in mind that there are two diseases and only two diseases which the World Health Assembly has committed itself to eradicate—guinea-worm disease and poliomyelitis. Guinea-worm eradication, with Don Hopkins as its brilliant and persuasive advocate and strategist, has been conducted with all due attention to surveillance, to community participation, to political commitment, and to research in shaping an evolving agenda. Despite this, it lags behind scheduled targets and it is clear that its successful conclusion will require a high degree of commitment and political skill. The outcome is not a foregone conclusion but I believe it can and will succeed.

[In 1999] poliomyelitis programmes have scarcely begun in those areas of Africa and south Asia which all but thwarted global smallpox eradication. Thus, the most difficult and problematical areas and years are still ahead, with programme implementation notably hampered by its reliance on a heat-labile vaccine whose efficacy leaves much to be desired and clumsy diagnostic tools. Fortunately, however, research has begun to appear on the programme's agenda. While we all hope that the programme will be successful, there is much yet to be learned and to be applied before success can be assured.

However, an international commitment has been made and high priority must be given to meeting these goals. A failure, especially in achieving poliomyelitis eradication, could as certainly call into question the credibility of the public health profession as did the collapse of the disastrous malaria eradication effort.

As we contemplate the future, is it necessary or even desirable to restrict ourselves to the narrow question of what disease should next be eradicated or eliminated? Through implementation of the smallpox, poliomyelitis and guinea-worm programmes, innovative breakthroughs have been made in organizing large-scale nationwide campaigns; in devising new methods for approaching and mobilizing communities; in developing effective national surveillance networks and in using the data in evolving better strategies; in fostering effective and relevant research programmes to facilitate disease control; and in mobilizing support at international, national and local levels.

I see these approaches as key steps in revolutionizing and revitalizing public health. Implicit in these new approaches is the setting of measurable goals and a willingness to look at all alternative methods for achieving them without assuming, as we so often have, that every intervention, every vaccine, every drug must somehow be directed or dispensed by some sort of primary health centre. These new initiatives and new approaches are of special relevance as we endeavour to deal with tuberculosis, leprosy, and micronutrient deficiencies such as iodine and Vitamin A. Likewise, use of albendazole, ivermectin and praziquantel on a strategically targeted community-wide basis could have a profound effect on many types of symptomatic parasitic disease. None of these are conditions to be eradicated in our lifetimes but they are diseases in which far more substantial progress could be made than we are now making while relying primarily on one-on-one traditional curative treatment. As time progresses, it may become apparent that certain of these diseases might warrant an eradication effort or might warrant one if better tools could be made available.

In looking to the future, however, I believe it is critical that we should not be blinded to a range of new public health programme paradigms by staring too fixedly at the blinding beacon of a few eradication dreams.

CHRONOLOGY

1546

Italian physician and poet Girolamo Fracastoro writes: "Contagion is an infection that passes from one thing to another." He recognizes that infections can be transmitted by contact with contaminated individuals, objects, and air.

1665

English chemist, mathematician, physicist, naturalist, and inventor Robert Hooke publishes *Micrographie*, drawings and observations of things viewed under a microscope. He describes the compartments in a slice of cork, calling them "cells."

1670s

Dutch merchant turned lens maker Antoni van Leeuwenhoek observes microorganisms and reports his observations to the Royal Society of London over the next fifty years.

1796

English physician Edward Jenner discovers a vaccination for smallpox by inoculation with cowpox pus. Jenner did not understand the cause of the disease or the immunity, but his observations and experiments led to a successful vaccine.

1840s

Hungarian physician Ignaz Semmelweis advises hand washing for physicians between all examinations, especially before childbirth. The incidence of childbed fever declines dramatically for those doctors who followed the advice.

Mid- to late 1800s

The Great Sanitary Awakening in Europe and America.

1854

English physician John Snow discovers that water is a mode of transmission for cholera. He subsequently stops a cholera epidemic by removing access to the contaminated water source.

1857

French chemist Louis Pasteur discovers fermentation.

1859

British naturalist Charles Darwin publishes his theory of natural selection and the origin of species.

1860s

Pasteur invents pasteurization to prevent spoilage of wine, beer, and milk.

1865

Pasteur begins to study silkworm diseases and establishes the basic rules of sterilization, or asepsis.

1867

British doctor Joseph Lister publishes his finding that carbolic acid is an antiseptic—it prevents wounds from becoming diseased. Over the next decade, Lister's aseptic techniques are adopted and enhanced throughout Europe and America.

1872

German botanist Ferdinand Cohn founds the science of bacteriology with the publication of a three-volume treatise describing, categorizing, and naming bacteria.

1876

German doctor Robert Koch publishes the complete etiology of the anthrax bacillus, which finally convinces critics that Pasteur's germ theory of disease is accurate.

1880

Pasteur demonstrates how protection against disease (chicken cholera) can be accomplished by inoculation with a weakened strain of the causative agent.

1881

Pasteur publicly proves the success of his anthrax vaccine on sheep.

1882

Koch presents irrefutable evidence that tuberculosis is caused by a specific bacillus. Russian microbiologist Dmitri Ivanowski publishes the first evidence that an infectious agent can pass through a porcelain filter.

1884

Koch published his postulates for proving disease causation. Danish bacteriologist Hans Christian Gram develops the Gram stain for differentiating between two major classes of bacteria based on their cell wall characteristics.

1885

Pasteur uses a rabies vaccine to prevent two boys from contracting rabies.

1888

The Pasteur Institute is established in France.

1890

German physician Emil von Behring, while working in Koch's laboratory, discovers the antitoxin for diphtheria and tetanus toxins. Over time he develops this into a cure for those with diphtheria and an immunization to prevent disease in others. Koch is made director of the newly established Institute for Infectious Diseases in Germany.

1891

The Lister Institute is established in England.

1898

Dutch microbiologist Martinus Beijerinck recognizes "soluble" living microbes, a term he applies to the discovery of tobacco mosaic virus. German bacteriologists Friedrich Loeffler and Paul Frosch prove that foot-and-mouth disease in livestock is caused by organisms tiny enough to pass through bacteriological filters and too small to be seen through a common microscope.

1901

U.S. Army surgeon major Walter Reed, along with the members of the Yellow Fever Commission, prove that mosquitos are the intermediate host for yellow fever, and that the agent of contagion is a filterable virus.

1912

German doctor Paul Ehrlich announces the discovery of an effective cure (salvarsan) for syphilis, the first specific chemotherapeutic agent for a bacterial disease.

1915

British bacteriologist Frederick Twort announces the discovery of bacteria-infecting viruses.

1918

Spanish flu pandemic is most devastating recorded global epidemic.

1928

Scottish bacteriologist Sir Alexander Fleming discovers penicillin.

1938

Australian pathologist Howard Florey and German-Jewish biochemist Ernst Chain come across Fleming's paper on penicillin while working at Oxford University in England. Their experiments lead to commercially available penicillin by 1942.

1943

Bacteriologists Oswald Avery, Colin MacLeod, and Maclyn Mc-Carty show that DNA is the carrier of genetic information.

1944

Rutgers University graduate student Albert Schatz, with the help of Elizabeth Bugie and working under Russian-born bacteriologist Selman Waksman, discovers streptomycin, which is effective against tuberculosis.

1946

The Communicable Disease Center, or CDC, opens as part of the U.S. Public Health Service (PHS).

1948

The World Health Organization (WHO) is established under the United Nations to promote and facilitate health to all people in the world.

1949

American microbiologist John Franklin Enders, virologist Thomas H. Weller, and physician Frederick Chapman Robbins develop a technique to grow poliovirus in test-tube cultures of human tissues—a new, practical tool for the isolation and study of viruses.

Early 1950s

Four common childhood vaccines exist: diphtheria, tetanus, pertussis, and smallpox. The first three are remedied with one vaccine, the DPT.

1951

The Epidemic Intelligence Service (EIS) is established within the CDC to respond to health emergencies and conduct national disease surveillance.

1952

American biologists Alfred Hershey and Martha Chase perform radioactive isotope experiments to confirm that only DNA is needed for viral replication. American doctor Jonas Salk discovers the polio vaccine and begins testing it.

1953
British biophysicist Francis Crick and American biologist James Watson describe the double-helical structure of DNA.

1957
The Asian flu pandemic strikes, but it is not as devastating as the 1918 pandemic.

1958
American doctor Albert Sabin independently discovers, tests, and develops a polio vaccine independently from Salk.

1968
The Hong Kong flu pandemic is the mildest pandemic to date.

1970
The Communicable Disease Center is renamed the Centers for Disease Control to reflect a broader mission in preventive health.

1976
CDC investigates an outbreak of illness in Philadelphia now called Legionnaire's disease. The following year, CDC researchers isolate the causative agent for this disease: *Legionella pneumophilia.* Ebola hemorrhagic fever is discovered.

1978
Smallpox is declared officially eliminated. It is the only microbial disease to ever have been deliberately eradicated.

1981
The first cases of a new disease, later called AIDS, are reported in the CDC's *Morbidity and Mortality Weekly Report (MMWR).*

1982
American neurologist Stanley Prusiner finds evidence that certain

diseases might be caused by a class of infectious proteins that he calls prions. The cause of Lyme disease is determined to be a bacteria carried by deer ticks.

1983
American doctor Robert Gallo and French doctor Luc Montagnier announce their discovery of the human immunodeficiency virus (HIV) believed to cause AIDS.

Mid- to late 1980s
Measles, mumps, and rubella (MMR) vaccine and polio vaccine are added to the list of common childhood vaccines. Smallpox had been removed from the list, so seven vaccines are common and six of them are combined in two sets of three (DPT and MMR). In the late 1980s, a meningitis vaccine (Hib) is added.

1990s
Multidrug-resistant tuberculosis bacteria (MDRTB) are discovered in the United States (1991) and other countries. Antibacterial soaps, hand sanitizers, kitchen gadgets, and children's toys begin to flood the market. Hepatitis B and chicken pox vaccines are added to the list of common childhood vaccines.

1993
An outbreak of an unexplained pulmonary illness from a previously unknown type of hantavirus, Sin Nombre virus (SNV), occurs in the southwestern United States.

1997
A new strain of flu in humans, influenza A (H5N1), the avian flu, is reported in Hong Kong.

2000
A pneumonia (pneumococcal) vaccine is added to the list of common childhood vaccines.

2002
Vancomycin-resistant staphylococci are discovered. Vancomycin is the drug of last defense against staph infections.

FOR FURTHER RESEARCH

Books

Nicholas Bakalar, *Where the Germs Are.* Hoboken, NJ: John Wiley, 2003.

Wayne Biddle, *A Field Guide to Germs.* New York: Henry Holt, 1995.

Thomas D. Brock, *Robert Koch: A Life in Medicine and Bacteriology.* Washington, DC: ASM, 1999.

Robert DeSalle, ed., *Epidemic! The World of Infectious Disease.* New York: New Press, 1999.

René J. Dubos, *Louis Pasteur: Free Lance of Science.* Boston: Little, Brown, 1950.

———, *Pasteur and Modern Science.* Boston: Little, Brown, 1960.

Brent Hoff and Carter Smith III, *Mapping Epidemics: A Historical Atlas of Disease.* New York: Franklin Watts, 2000.

Paul de Kruif, *Microbe Hunters.* New York: Harcourt, Brace, 1926.

Joshua S. Lederberg, ed., *Encyclopedia of Microbiology.* 2nd edition. New York: Academic Press, 1997.

William H. McNeill, *Plagues and Peoples.* New York: Doubleday, 1976.

Judith Miller, William Broad, and Stephen Engelberg, *Germs: Biological Weapons and America's Secret War.* New York: Simon & Schuster, 2001.

Sherwin B. Nuland, *The Doctor's Plague: Germs, Childbed Fever, and the Strange Story of Ignaz Semmelweis.* New York: W.W. Norton, 2003.

Richard Rhodes, *Deadly Feasts: Tracking the Secrets of a Terrifying New Plague.* New York: Simon & Schuster, 1997.

Philip M. Tierno, *The Secret Life of Germs: What They Are, Why We Need Them, and How We Can Protect Ourselves Against Them.* New York: Atria, 2004.

Periodicals

Joel Achenbach, "Our Friend the Plague: Can Germs Keep Us Healthy?" *National Geographic*, November 2003.

Madeline Drexler, "Deadly Crossovers of the Darwinian Divide," *Boston Globe*, June 2, 2003.

Thomas W. Grein et al., "Rumors of Disease in the Global Village: Outbreak Verification," *Emerging Infectious Diseases*, March/April 2000.

Garry Hamilton, "Why We Need Germs," *Ecologist*, June 2001.

Jerold M. Lowenstein, "Can We Wipe Out Disease?" *Discover*, November 1992.

New Scientist, "For Whose Eyes Only: How Do You Preserve Scientific Freedom and Combat Terrorism?" January 18, 2003.

Michael Precker, "A Nasty Brush with Germs," Knight Ridder/Tribune News Service, September 4, 2004.

Peter Radetsky, "The Good Virus," *Discover*, November 1996.

Carol Reeves, "Can Rhetorical Momentum Influence Agreement in Science?" *Scientist*, January 13, 2003.

Michael Shnayerson, "The Killer Bug: A Lethal New Mutation of the Wily Staph Bacterium Is Proving Resistant to the Best Antibiotic in the Drawer. Can a Vaccine Stop It?" *Fortune*, September 30, 2002.

David Stipp, "Germs Make the Man: Your Body Is Teeming with Trillions of Infectious Microbes. That's a Very Good Thing," *Fortune*, January 20, 2003.

Paul Thagard, "The Concept of Disease: Structure and Change," *Communication and Cognition*, vol. 29, 1996. http://cogsci. uwaterloo.ca/Articles/Pages/Concept.html.

Bob Weinhold, "Infectious Disease: The Human Costs of Our Environmental Errors," *Environmental Health Perspectives*, January 2004.

Web Sites

American Society for Microbiology, www.microbeworld.org. The ASM is the largest single life science society, composed of over forty-two thousand scientists and health professionals. It promotes research and training in the microbiological sciences and assists communication between scientists, policy makers, and the public. The site provides definitions, explanations, and current issues related to microbiology. There are links for kids, educators, and scientists.

Biosecurity and Bioterrorism: Biodefense Strategy, Practice, and Science, www.biosecurityjournal.com. This online journal presents opinion and research articles related to the emerging field of biodefense.

Cells Alive!, www.cellsalive.com. This Web site by James A. Sullivan presents information on cell biology, microbiology, immunology, and microscopy. It also contains film and computer-enhanced images of many germs and other microbes.

Founders of Biological and Medical Sciences, www.foundersof science.net. Professor of biochemistry David V. Cohn created this site to commemorate five brilliant scientists of the past: Edward Jenner, Louis Pasteur, Robert Koch, Ignaz Semmelweis, and Joseph Baron Lister. The site contains biographies, histories, and commentaries about these great men and their contributions to science and controversies with their peers.

INDEX